I PISSED IN S⬤ME GUY'S Bottle Of...

A LIFE SPENT RIGHTING LIFE'S WRONGS

RICK LESLIE

"Rick's wandering mind latches onto subjects firmly on the edge but are actually right in the middle of our daily existence."

Mike Leonard, former NBC News feature reporter

"This book often reads like a comedy routine. (It's) lightheartedness is easy to appreciate."

Kirkus Reviews

What others are saying about Rick and his book.

"I pray this book never sees the light of day."

Pamela Leslie, wife

"What kind of a father tells his son to drop out of college to tour with a band? I missed my one chance to become a doctor."

Scott Leslie, concert promoter

"It wasn't easy growing up with him. He spit in my mouth."

Jamie Leslie, music agent

"The best advice he ever gave me was to move far, far away."

Alison Leslie Corkery, Arizona resident

"I don't know where I went wrong."

Essie Leslie, deceased mother

"Yes, I kissed him. But I threw up three seconds later."

Drunk high school classmate

"This isn't writing. It's more like learning disgusting secrets."

Miss Nora, former English teacher

"Doesn't surprise me that he wound up plagiarizing his life."

Sgt. Zweitz, Rick's 5th grade teacher

"I've known Rick for 42 years. One of them was pretty good."

Dick Salyer, Sr. VP in advertising

"Only an idiot would use the word pissing in a title. Who's going to ask for a book like that in a bookstore or library."

Anonymous Book Buyer

"Do not listen to anything he's written. It'll mess up your mind."

Dr. Baker, Rick's psychiatrist

"Don't buy this book! It's just one more Rick Leslie scam to make money."

Lee Schneider, best friend

"When we heard he's planning on selling his book at his funeral, rather than be eulogized, we walked away fast."

Simon & Schuster Editor

"The author stole this unbelievably great book from me. He may own the copyright. But I wrote the whole damn thing."

Rick's alter ego

This book is dedicated to me.
For without me, this book would
never have been written.

The Most Peculiar Chapters of My Life

Here lies the truth…

Me

It took me seventy-plus years to write this book.
(How to be a nobody. Yet wind up a somebody.)

HI, I'M THE GUY WHO wrote this book. It's a memoir. I hate memoirs. Especially ones written by some nobody like me. I mean, why should anybody give a damn about my life?

I barely graduated college.

I was never what you'd call a runaway success.

And, to this day, you'd have to dig deep to find any Google hits about me.

Sadly, my lone claim to fame is the brief appearance I made on page eighty-seven of the New York Times bestseller *Ride of Our Lives*. And, if I stretch things a bit, the dozen or so times my hands and feet appeared on national TV.

Little else separates me from the run-of-the-mill crowd, other than I've lived my entire life along the outside edges of normal human behavior. I don't really like living there, but I had no choice in the matter.

It's who I am, who I've always been, and who I'll always be.

I tell you this because you can't read the stories of my life without recognizing the fundamental truth of my existence. Sometimes I feel like I was conceived inside a scrambled egg, birthed only to take on contrarian views to popular opinions solely for argument's sake.

A few cases in point:

I sympathize with the wealthy for being hated by the masses.

I purposely eat foods I don't enjoy to keep my weight in check.

And I prefer flying after plane crashes because it increases my odds of survival.

Like it or not, you're just now beginning to know who I am.

It's this sort of quirky thinking that has always set me apart from others. One or two broken chromosomes might have contributed to my offbeat nature as well—the result of a father stationed in Nagasaki right after the bomb had been dropped. And who fathered me soon after.

But the uptake is, those possible mutated genes of his might have genetically provided me with a unique take on everyday shit.

It's as good of an explanation as you're going to get from me.

I think of it as a creative gift—a gift I enjoy using. Though I admit it did come at the expense of living my whole life in *la la land*—a mentally imbalanced place to reside.

Most notably when you're a kid.

Sure, I had friends. But even friends' loyalties can be put to the test when you're the one doing the testing.

Like you can't pull down your pants at a crowded bowling alley without jaws dropping.

I have no idea what I was thinking then. I think that was the problem.

You also can't spend an entire semester in fifth grade facing the back wall. Yet feel as if you're in the in-crowd.

I guess child abuse didn't exist back then.

And you certainly can't ditch day camp, park yourself under a tree all day, and hum mindless melodies buried deep in your imagination without expecting eye-rolls from the pretty girl walking past.

"Are you okay," she might have asked?

In those days, I didn't realize my thinking might be somewhat skewed toward the weird side. Looking at myself from the inside out, I made perfect sense to myself. I mean, it's not like I spoke in tongues or anything.

I just spoke in burps sometimes.[1]

FYI: That gaseous faux pas resulted in my third-grade teacher escorting me to the girl's washroom as punishment. Not wishing to discuss this matter further, all I'll type on the subject is best summed up this way.

That was when I first learned to piss sitting down.[2]

Why were no naughty girls in my class forced to go standing up?

A much bigger *why*, however, is why so many people tell me they've never known anyone like me.

And *why* they say my life as a nobody is in fact noteworthy.

I sometimes wonder why myself.

It's because… It's because…

Hell, if I knew why they say it, I might want to stop being me right now. And if I wasn't me, you'd probably stop reading this second. Out of boredom.

And you'd ask for your money back. Which would be a serious mistake, because my memoir is both interesting and entertaining. It includes over seventy years of strange happenings, weird thoughts, odd situations, and many unfortunate misbehaviors. I write the latter because the comings and goings of my life stretch way beyond the imagination of typical everyday happenstance.

Yes, some wacky stuff has occurred in my life that likely has never cropped up in yours.

Unless you've also been caught counterfeiting.

I've also had many outrageous ideas arise out of nowhere, like going back to college at age sixty-one to get low-cost student health insurance.

Oh, did you solve the healthcare crisis too?

And my thirst for revenge often goes beyond the unthinkable.

Please don't tell me you've also made some jerk drink your bodily fluids.

At this point in my life, if I did it, I'm telling it. Here you'll get the whole truth and nothing but.

As well as all the juicy details a pleasure-seeker could desire.

Fact is, only the blurbs at the beginning of this book under *What others are saying about Rick and his book* are made up. Though brutally frank in their assessments of me, I had to write each one myself because I couldn't trust the people who know me best to write the truth about me.

And let's face it, true stuff is always better than made-up shit—some of which might lead you to believe I'm less than an empathetic person. Perhaps an accurate portrayal, but only if you put the emphasis on the *pathetic* part of the word.

By now you're probably thinking I'm a total nutcase. I assure you I'm not. My credentials are impeccable—worthy of someone far more successful than I ever was.

Upon graduating college in 1971, I fingerpicked my way through the Chicago folk music scene, made final callbacks for the musical *Hair,* recorded a slightly-less-than-hit single for *Boogie Man Records,* and sang on the last *You Deserve a Break Today* ad campaign for McDonald's.

Sounds impressive, if I do write so myself.

The problem was the music business wasn't doing me any favors so far as a promising economic future goes, best demonstrated by the impulse that overcame me one afternoon in 1975 as I crossed the Chicago River.

That's when I first felt the urge to fling my guitar off the Michigan Avenue bridge. I took that as an omen to get out of music and into something more profitable.

That something turned out to be advertising.

Over the next ten years and four jobs, I wrote hundreds of commercials and print ads for dozens of products. Everything from perfumes, candies and breakfast cereals to cat foods, sporting goods and fried chicken.

I even did a golf club commercial in which Mickey Mantle hit the first—and only—fair ball out of Yankee Stadium.

And then came the day I carelessly flirted with OJ's wife Nicole on a "Happy Cat" cat food TV shoot.[3] Her lack of interest in me was why I lived long enough to pursue a new life-changing opportunity that had come out of the blue. I landed a dream job at NBC News producing Mike Leonard's humorous feature stories on the Today show.

During my cross-country travels, I rode with the Mounties, was exposed to cosmic dust at NASA, and danced to the beat of Cajun music in the Bayou.

Chances are you've seen some of my work on TV. Much of it was nominated for awards, like the documentaries I produced on the Kennedy assassination and on pedophile priests.

And much of it wasn't.

Let's be honest, nobody does great work all the time, but…

Since my retirement in 2008, I've made people laugh without being funny, had my creative non-fiction published in top literary magazines, and became a professional storyteller—performing my true-life misadventures in front of live audiences. If that doesn't convince you I'm no dilly-dally dilettante, maybe this will. The most intimate parts of my life are funny, pitiful, vengeful, absurd, but most of all, educational.

Educational, in the sense that I've learned many important lessons as I've journeyed through life. And now I pass that accumulated wisdom on to you through the many life-changing chapters in this book.

Most are humorous. A couple are sad. But I promise you none are boring.

Well, maybe one or two are snoozers if you count the sleepless night I spent at a zoo.

Or the fact that I fear my own dreams.

But the most interesting aspect of my memoir is that it's not really a memoir. It's only disguised as one.

Truth is, *I Pissed in Some Guy's Bottle Of...* is a how-to book filled with everything you need to know to right all the wrongs done to you—as well as all the wrongs you did to others.

Read it and you'll learn how to live life on your own terms and so much more. Including...

How to turn the table on others.

How to get the last laugh on somebody who thought they got it.

How to be funny without being funny.

How to negotiate a better price.

How to stay sane in a world which isn't.

How to get even with assholes.

How to speed without getting tickets.

How to accept an imperfect life.

And how to stick it to the man.

The asshole deserves it.

You shouldn't need any more reason than that to buy it. Other than it's also the perfect book for people who don't like to read. It's fast, breezy, and doesn't use too many big words.

Finally, if you promise to keep it a secret, I'll reveal the ending right now as an added incentive to begin chapter one.

In the end, I die.[4]

What could be a better opening than that?

I think I may have one on the next page.

---

1. My favorite burps of all time were the twin, double-burp accents I provided for *The Blue Danube* in third-grade music class. I eventually became so adept at swallowing air that I subsequently learned to burp entire sentences. Like the one I'm doing this minute. I just burped, "It's harder to burp in my late seventies than it was at nine."

2. To this day, I piss more accurately sitting down than standing up. I never miss the bowl when my ass is on the seat.

3. I cast O.J. Simpson's baby daughter Sydney in a Happy Cat TV commercial. That's why Nicole was on the set. Her murder remains solved.

4. In lieu of flowers, a donation may be made to *I Pissed in Some Guy's Bottle Of...*

1

I caressed a naked woman without touching her.
(How to turn a sexual fantasy into a masturbatory reality.)

Unnatural Act I, Obscene 1

I THOUGHT ABOUT my mother.

I wrote a song in my head.

I recited my ABC's backward.

I tried to do everything I could to get my mind off the woman standing inches from me, but I couldn't help myself. I had to look. Compelled actually. She was stark naked, and hey, I was a guy. A young guy back in late 1972—hadn't yet met my wife—and I was nervous I might embarrass myself by-well—uh—you know why.

Fifteen minutes earlier the girl had been a total stranger. Though that's not totally true, since I couldn't help but notice her the moment she walked through the door. Her name was Rocky. Or so her I.D. badge indicated ten minutes prior to my meeting her.

I can only describe her as a Greek Goddess of some kind. Most likely, Aphrodite.

Or maybe an alluring Siren.

Whatever she was, Rocky definitely set off a five-alarm fire inside me.

She had long, dark, wavy hair falling halfway down her back, wore black leather hip boots running halfway up her thighs, and she was tall and lean and wore tight, tight jeans that made her look armed and dangerous.

No way she was innocent.

By the way she carried herself, she could have been a fashion model. Five minutes later I learned that's exactly what she was. But presently, she was also an actress cast in a local Chicago musical based on a famous Greek tragedy. At the initial rehearsal, we both listened as the director filled us in on the plot.

That's right, I had a role in the show too. I had sung and danced like a dumb chicken at my audition. A rooster, if I'm going to be forthright.

And what does every rooster want? A hen, of course.

Obscene 2

You can imagine my excitement when opportunistic chance paired me with Rocky. The director had told the cast of thirty-one that we were going to warm up with a few theatrical exercises. Exercise one was to grab our partner's hand and jump up and down in unison.

Exercise two was to get naked.

"Okay, kids, take off all your clothes and face your partner," said the director.

I can't remember undressing. I guess watching Rocky disrobe was far more deserving of my attention. But no ogling was permitted, so I feigned disinterest. After all, I didn't want her to find me a total creep.

Yet, I wasn't above sneaking a few casual peeks as she unbuttoned her blouse, pulled off her boots, and unzipped her jeans. Of most interest, though, were the few promising and hopeful seconds it took to remove her bra and panties.

That was when I started to think about my mother.

Unnatural Act II, Obscene 1

If you haven't yet surmised that this musical had a nude scene, you haven't been paying close enough attention. So, how's this for an attention-getter?

Rocky was staring at my thingamajig. That's because I had looked her straight in the eyes to avoid looking at her tangled, black triangle below. It was a mistake.

Unable to sustain my gaze, she averted her eyes and cast them downward. It made her appear a bit self-conscious, (which I most definitely liked). But I could only hope she wasn't laughing to herself about the size of my equipment. Be that as it may, don't all men wish that at moments like these, (though it's impossible to judge how many men have had moments like these).

"Now gently stroke your partner without actually touching one another," the director continued.

Oh my, I thought, concerned with what might *come* next.

My fingers cautiously traced Rocky's body. Careful not to make contact, I closed in on her shoulders and back, her breasts and tummy, and her buttocks and pubic hair. It was all so, so—

So, I made up a melody in my head to keep my mind occupied on other things.

But that wasn't easy to do, seeing that Rocky was doing the exact same thing to me that I was doing to her. We were mirror images of ourselves. Entirely in sync, engaged fully in gear.

And poetically conjoined in the artful act of nude—*if not lewd*—body outlining.

When my hands sought out her—her—

And her hands cupped my—my—

She—she, I—I—

I recited my ABC's backward. But couldn't get further than T.

Obscene 2

I must write that many of you readers have dirty, filthy minds. Folks, this was a theatrical exercise, so cool it.

Even if I found it impossible to do so.

My heart was pounding faster and faster with every surge of chills that ran up and down my spine. But this was show business—most definitely *show* business—for we showed each other everything we had: Nipples, balls, breasts, bellies, asses, cock, pussy, thighs and pubes.

All.

For the sake.

Of art.

Or was it?

I looked over at the director, also standing naked.

'Naked? Why was he naked?" I wondered.

In his mid-forties, he had chosen a partner like the rest of us had. He stood in front of her with a big gut and a small erection. Apparently, he had plotted this whole thing out, arranging his little musical so the play's *erotic* plot and his *seductive* ploy would climax together in an onstage/offstage dénouement.

The director's deception had taken my mind momentarily off Rocky. By the time I got back into the right mood, the routine had finished.

As Rocky and I dressed, I smiled warmly at her. She blushed and demurely returned my flirtatious grin. Our theatrical training had most definitely softened her up. It would have the exact opposite effect on me soon after.

At rehearsal's end, Rocky went her way and I went mine. I hadn't spoken one word to her. I might have if I had continued with the show. But before I left for the day, the director had named his female partner the leading lady. When I heard her sing, I mumbled half under my breath, "My God, she can't sing."

Somehow this girl's absence of talent diminished my own. I didn't want to be a part of any show that embarrassed me by featuring a less-than-stellar-star. Rocky or no Rocky, I called up the next day and did the only thing I could.

I quit.

To my way of thinking, nobody should ever attach themselves to mediocrity. It makes you look mediocre too.

Obscene 3

However, my memory of Rocky—and the ten "naked" minutes we spent together—lingers to this day.

I recently told my wife about the time I caressed a nude woman without touching her. (I pretty much tell her everything.) She asked me to do the same to her as an experiment. When I finished, she gave me the flirtiest smile ever. I asked her what *that* was all about.

"Oh, my God," she said. "I felt it. It was like a delicate breeze kissing my skin."

I didn't tell my wife what was on my mind right then. She may have thought it was sex. But I'm a dirty old man now, so what I was really thinking was…

Oh, boy! Had Rocky sensed my hands moving up and down her nude body that day?

That possibility plastered a smug smile on my blemish-free, majority unwrinkled, seventy-plus-year-old face. I headed to the library soon after to rewrite the ending to this chapter.

And to think about how fortunate I am to have a wife who understands me.

2

I picked up dog doo with my bare hands.
(How to show someone you love them, inside and out.)

IT REALLY WASN'T DOG doo that I picked up.

In this real-life tale of affection, I've substituted dog doo for human excrement, though I'm not sure dog doo can be used as a metaphor or allegory for people poo. Even if they are sort of the same thing.

Perhaps they're more like similes.

I like similes. They're—like—simple. But I abhor metaphors and allegories. It goes back to high school when linguistic tricks usually went over my head.

As they did when I plodded through literature like *Wuthering Heights* and *David Copperfield*—two books I found as confusing as road maps, pardon my analogy. (Or is it a metaphor?)

Why write in cryptic code, I've often wondered, when you can write exactly what you mean? Does the use of metaphors and allegories really make writing more enjoyable? If that's true, how come most everybody dislikes reading Shakespeare?

Just writing his name gives me the heebie-jeebies. Only English teachers, English majors, the literati, and intellectuals appreciate the guy. I can't imagine what interpreting his works must do to ordinary folks. His plays are impossible to understand. Who can read that stuff anyway? If you ask me, his words were meant *to be* heard and *not to be* read.[1]

Call me ignorant if you must, but I loved Mel Gibson in *Hamlet*. He played the role like he played Martin Riggs in *Lethal Weapon*. The closest Shakespeare ever got to writing a good buddy comedy was *The Two Gentlemen of Verona*.

But I digress.

The point I was trying to make paragraphs ago was not literary in kind. It was more about the kind of person I am. A sensitive man. Someone who cares deeply about other people's feelings.

And for that reason, I exchanged dog doo for human excrement in this memory to avoid causing someone the embarrassment of being outed.

On the other hand, I do like to make my words as enjoyable to read as possible. So let me move on by writing that there's someone special in my life that I love much more than my dog. But for privacy's sake, I'll refer to her by my dog's name—Winnie the Poodle.

Or Winnie the Pooh for short.

Or for a more succinct union of poodle and pooh and dog and doo, Winnie the Poo.

Like so many other two-legged female creatures, Winnie has basic needs like eating, sleeping, and going out a lot. Being the kind and understanding man that I am, I take her to movies, plays, restaurants, ballets and symphonies. I also let her romp in the backyard three times a day.

In return, she shows her affection by licking me all over. I've always loved that about Winnie. In a metaphorical sort of way, I guess.

But doo is doo any way you *pood* it.[2] That's true whether it comes from Winnie, ET or Benito Mussolini (aka BM). It's nothing but waste consisting of fat, water and protein. As harmless as those molecules may be, human excrement, if swallowed, can result in a deadly case of E. coli.

15

However, many of the ingredients in feces can also be used to treat diseases like MS, IBS, Crohn's and Parkinson's. In those instances, waste is *not* a waste. It's of great benefit to humanity.

But like everything else in life, you have to take the good with the bad.

Much like marriage is for better *and* for worse.

Sometimes on the same day.

Like the day Winnie and I went on vacation years ago, (though the real Winnie hadn't been born yet).

I had made reservations at an upscale hotel. Upon checking in, we went up to our room. It was bright and cheerful, had a décor that can best be described as welcoming, and came complete with a large balcony overlooking the pool.

How were we to know there was a big problem with the room?

Specifically, the plumbing.

When Winnie said she had to go right after we walked in, she went. If she had gone on the lawn, it wouldn't have been a problem. Some maintenance guy would have mowed it into fertilizer clumps and that would have been the end of it. But Winnie had used the toilet, a most peculiar thing for a dog to do.

Except in the imagination of a writer.

Whoa. Did I just imagine myself a writer?

However, the toilet wouldn't flush, a necessary feature to send dog doo on its ride to the sewers. So it sat in the water *doo-ing* nothing.

In a normal situation, one might call the front desk to have someone fix the toilet. But Winnie was bashful in times past, and prim and proper like poodles from Boston are prone to be. She considered dirty things a private matter and was plenty anxious about a total stranger seeing her poo.

Myself excluded, even if I am a stranger to her sometimes.

I looked down at *it*. And then looked up at her as if to say, what do you want me to do about it?

She neither spoke nor whimpered.

Instead, Winnie looked up at me with her big, blue, puppy dog eyes pleading—perhaps begging—for help. I'm a sucker for those kinds of eyes. It left me with no choice other than to answer her distress call. She needed to be saved like a baby bird with a broken wing.

My simile made her smile like a burped baby on Similac.

But how does one handle a situation such as this?

I did it the only way I knew how.

I went to the bathroom, swathed my hand with toilet paper, and reached deep into the water. That's when I discovered that tissue paper dipped in water turns into a flimsy nothing on contact.

In effect, the doo was lying in my bare hand.

"Now what?" I said to myself as the "brown blimplette"[3] drooled droplets into the toilet bowl below.

I began to swear at hotel housekeeping for giving us a bum room with a broken toilet, and for placing the onus on me to correct it. But what good was that going to do? Winnie was wronged by them and it was up to me to make things right.

For a second, I considered tossing the shit into the sink and running hot water to melt it. But I had to use that same sink later to clean my contact lenses. Reevaluating the situation, I reached an executive decision, and marched out of the bathroom with dog doo in hand, double-timing it past the bed, dresser and easy chair until I slid open the door to the balcony, stepped to the railing, and let 'er fly.

It landed with a soft plop in the flowerbed below. On the edge of a patio belonging to the hotel guests beneath us.

One could only hope a sweet puppy dog had checked into that room as well.

As disgusting as it was, I only mention this incident now because Winnie's doo stood for something far more substantial than poo.

It was an expression of love.

If you don't believe me, ask your loved one if he, she, or what-have-you would dare do something like I did. They may say yes now—*sure thing, dear*—but everyone says yes when they are under no (water) pressure.

Me? I rose to the occasion when it counted. The proof lies in the *poo-dung*. It says I love my Winnie as I would a wife. The two are much more alike than you might think, you know.

As for readers unable to accept this book as great literature, the dog doo in this story is an allegory. It stands for all the other crap we humans have to deal with.

Now go wash your hands before reading on.

_____

1. When I was performing around Chicago in the 1970s, a sleazy music agent said he was interested in signing me. I thought it would be cool to have an agent, so I met him at his office. The first thing out of his mouth was how I needed a gimmick. He proposed changing my name to Billy Shakespeare. I told him I'd think about it but never did. My lyrics weren't that good.

2. This chapter uses a lot of groan-worthy puns. Sorry for putting them in. It makes me look like an immature boy who hasn't yet reached poo-berty.

3. *Blimplette* is a word I made up to represent the more delicate nature of the female bowel movement.

3

I know how to speed without getting tickets.
(How to outsmart the police when caught in a speed trap.)

I CAN'T COUNT THE number of speeding tickets I got between the ages of sixteen and fifty-five.

But I can total the number of times a cop stopped me and didn't write one out.

Zero. Zilch. Nada.

I have nobody to blame for that but myself.

I was guilty every time. The punishment—a ticket—was always warranted. It was the price I paid for driving too fast. I have no right to complain about any of the tickets I received. That doesn't mean I liked getting them, though. But who am I to argue with the traffic laws in this country? As you know, I'm a complete nobody.

However, I'm also somebody good at coming up with unusual creative solutions.

Because of that, I was able to join a new class of speeders who never get ticketed. It's a class of one.

Me.

I'm the only person on this Earth who's beaten the American traffic citation system at their own game. It's almost like I've been handed a free get-out-of-jail card for breaking the law.

However, the methodology I employ to escape the punishment of ticket-happy officers doesn't necessarily make me the sort of guy you'd want to hang out with.

It goes like so. I get inside their heads and play games with their minds.

There are dozens of other reasons to avoid me. But why raise further issues of my preternatural behavior now?

Am I wrong to manipulate the *hoi police* to my own advantage?

Maybe.

But I'd like to think my solutions to life's problems usually wind up a win-win for all concerned. Just know that I'm not writing this book to make you believe I'm a nice person, even though most everybody thinks I am.

But they don't know me like you now do.

No, this life-lesson isn't about morality.

Or ethics.

Or even traffic laws.

I just want to pass on whatever remaining torch of knowledge I carry before the light eternally dims. So really, what's the harm in using a little reverse psychology to wangle myself out of a speeding ticket?

That's how I felt prior to putting my system to work for the first time in 2002. I was speeding down Sheridan Road in north suburban Chicago when I saw a cop car hidden behind the hedges lining a driveway. I was caught red-handed.

Now I could have done what every other driver does in that situation—continue driving until the squad car pulled me over. But I opted for the *unexpected* instead.[1] (In the mind of the police officer if not by me.) I employed what my family calls the "Leslie Maneuver," a manipulative ploy that pops into my head from time to time to get myself out of jams. In this case…

I stopped before the cop stopped me.

But the cop didn't know that until he turned on his "red and blues," pulled out of the driveway and nearly rear-ended me. That's because I had stopped just a few feet beyond the same hedges he had used to hide his squad car.

In my rearview mirror, I could see his expression change from astonishment to bewilderment as he walked over to my car. My sudden stop had disarmed him—and had straightaway turned his mindset from foe to friend.

It amazes me that nobody had thought of doing this before. By pulling over before the police officer could pull out into traffic, I wasn't just admitting defeat. I was surrendering before the battle had begun. I was the one-in-a-million driver taking full responsibility for his or her actions. It left no doubt that I would be the highlight of this cop's typical day.

"Honey, you wouldn't believe what happened to me today. A speeder stopped before I stopped him."

That doesn't happen too often, you know.

Instinctively, I knew I would be the one driver he'd never forget.[2] And that had to work to my advantage. My gut said he'd have to go easy on me because I had just made *his* job easy. I just about expected a little polite police applause from him for being such an upright citizen.

Well done, sir. Very well done. Clap-clap.

As I rolled down the window, the officer was shaking his head in disbelief.

"Nobody's ever done that before," he said. "I'm not going to ticket you. You're too honest." And with that, I drove off. Ostensibly proving that attitude counts for something when breaking the law.

Since then, I've sped—and stopped—five other times. And five more times it's worked. I suppose you could say my system is time-tested—and highway approved.

Even under the most extreme conditions.

Like the time I was going ninety-seven mph in a seventy zone on Route 65 in Indiana. I passed the cop tucked behind the overpass in a blur. I knew he had me on radar, so I immediately pulled off onto the shoulder before he could merge into traffic.

When the officer caught up to me a minute later, he shook his head the same way the first cop had. He even apologized when he said he couldn't let me off scot-free.

"You know," he said. "I'm supposed to take drivers into the station when they're going twenty-five over the limit. The best I can do is to put you down for going eleven over and issue a warning."

A warning ticket for going ninety-seven?

I managed to keep a straight face, but I was beaming on the inside. Life is so much better when you're the one coming out on top.

So next rainy day when you're going seventy-five in a sixty zone—but it feels like you're only going fifty-five—push the needle up to eighty.

But before you do, always remember...

STOP BEFORE THE COP STOPS YOU!

It's my way of righting the wrong that speeders perpetrate on flustered police officers every day.

My next challenge is to figure out how to get out of all the parking tickets I've gotten since I started writing this book at my local library. The final count: two hundred and twenty-five dollars.

Nobody said writing was going to be easy.

---

1. I use the word *unexpected*—and its many variations—a total of sixteen times in this book. It's not due to a limited vocabulary on my part. I could have used other substitute words such as atypical, exceptional, surprising, unanticipated, unfamiliar, unforeseen, unpredictable and so on. But I wanted to drive home a point about the benefits of doing the *unexpected*. It's the central theme of this book. And a well-advised course of action to take. Doing the *unexpected* makes you stand out from the crowd. It makes you impossible to forget.

2. Vince Kaman was an art rep in Chicago who sold his clients' illustrative talents to ad agency art directors. As a copywriter, I barely knew the guy and never had any dealings with him. I should have forgotten him long ago. Yet I still remember Vince to this day. That's because forty-some years ago I was having lunch with a few friends when Vince unexpectedly slapped down a twenty on the table and said, "Boys, lunch is on me today." I looked up and said, "Vince, you don't have to do that." To which, he replied, "I do if I want you to remember me." Lesson learned.

4

I didn't learn to write until I was twenty-nine.
(How to be a writer, even if you've failed English.)

I LEARNED TO READ thanks to *Dick and Jane,* a series of early childhood reading books.

"See Spot run. Run, Spot, run."

It was easy. But I'm ashamed to admit that I didn't learn to write until I was twenty-nine. I must have been sick the days they taught writing in grade school because I knew nothing of sentences.

Except for those in TV courtroom dramas.

I had no regard for punctuation.

I was often tardy because I was too busy thinking of malapropisms.

And nobody told me what a paragraph was so I was never sure where one ended and another began. That made all paragraphs stupid in my mind.

How was I to know I might be the stupid one? A cursory review of my earliest report cards indicates I had all the tools to be a writer. I was a finalist in classroom spelling bees and had a flair for cursive—writing the ABC's with a flowing and graceful feminine touch.

Yet I struggled to write anything that made much sense. Often relying on clumsy language that ran on and on without making a single point.

Other than the periods at the end of sentences.

But then came a breakthrough my freshman year of high school. I got a B on an English paper, my first B ever. It almost felt like I had gotten an A. (Perhaps a precursor of grade inflation to come.) I was absolutely thrilled by this sudden turn of events. But my joy was short-lived.

The next day I discovered I was in remedial English.

I figured if school teachers considered me a lost cause, who was I to argue? From that day forth, I avoided writing assignments any way I could.

Obviously, being the writer I am today, stringing together a coherent sentence was never beyond my capabilities. I just didn't get what writing was about. Thus, I failed English. Twice. Once in junior high and once in high school. Was it my fault? Or the fault of educators? Whatever the cause, it led to a sizable gap in my education—one I was unlikely to overcome.

Especially after scoring a lowly 442 on the verbal section of the SAT's.

Need I add that my vocabulary was bottom basement too?

Yet I became a writer. How the hell did I turn things around?

It was because I found the right teacher.

Except my teacher was no teacher. He was Mike Lubow, a creative director at a large ad agency in town. Though I couldn't write, I told him I wanted to become a copywriter.

My wish hadn't come out of left field, though. The idea had been planted in my brain the previous night while playing poker. One of the players—knowing I was unemployed, but wrongfully assuming I could write—suggested I go into advertising.

"It's easy," he said. "And you get to have martinis at lunch."

That's all it took to send me scurrying to Mike's office in search of a future beyond the dry-cleaning business—an offer my father-in-law had proposed a year earlier. Though I trusted *dad* was making an honest assessment of my abilities, I considered his lack of faith in me disturbing.

25

In fairness to him, however, it's hard to have faith in anyone not accomplishing much of anything.

But by replacing my fading—and failing—singer/songwriter career with a job requiring a similar use of imagination, I had a chance to prove him and all other naysayers wrong. Without Mike's help, there was little chance of that happening.

Perhaps I should mention that Mike's wife would have killed him if he hadn't met with me. She was my sister. That saddled my brother-in-law with a family obligation. He *had* to turn me into a copywriter.

It began with Mike telling me I needed to dream up a bunch of make-believe print ads to wow ad executives. A week later I returned to his office, ads in hand. He perused the work I'd done and, in as nice a tone as he could muster, said, "Maybe you should become a truck driver."

Ouch!

As I headed out the door, upset by the spit balling insult he had hurled, Mike called me back into his office. For what, I wondered? A consolation prize for dummies?

"Look, I didn't mean to be so hard on you," he said. "But there's nothing more I can teach you than this." He then summed up the aggregate of communications with this brief catchphrase.

"I don't get it… Aha, I get it now… Oh, neat. I love this."

That's when I learned what good writing is all about.

It's a continuous flow of "mystery presented." (*I don't get it.*)

Followed by "mystery solved." (*Aha, I get it now.*)

With a surprise twist at the end to reward the reader. (*Oh, neat. I love this.*)

It was all I needed to prove Mike's truck driver comment was way off base.

I suddenly got it. All of it.

The rain in Spain stays mainly on the plain…By George, I've got it!

Not just advertising. But how to take control of my life. How to create a new identity for myself. How to be anything I wanted to be.

Mysterious? Easy.

Interesting? No problem.

Cool? Nothing to it[1].

I tell you, I could write a whole self-help book on this subject. But for now, I'll stick to writing this one.

Now where was I? (Insert pre-dementia moment.) Oh, yeah.

Yes, the above process forces people to become involved in whatever you communicate. Whether it be about yourself or your writings. And leaves them wanting more. Why? Because you entertained them, silly. And, since time immemorial, people like to hang with people they find entertaining.

I became a writer that day.

Though many readers may disagree.

Three days later I went back to Mike's office with a half dozen new pretend ads—all potential award-winners. Bowled over by the work I'd done, he called an agency friend of his, who called another agency friend, who called another agency friend. The following day I was hired at Leo Burnett, one of the largest ad agencies in the world. It happened that quick.[2]

Today, Mike says he didn't do anything to turn me into a writer. That I had it in me all along. Maybe that's true. But I also know I had an *accidental mentor* to bring it out.

Most kids under twenty-nine years of age aren't so fortunate.

But whose fault is that?

---

1. *"I don't get it...Aha, I get it now...Oh, neat. I love this."* is more than a communications philosophy. As Robert Greene wrote in *Psychology Today*, "The moment people feel they know what to expect from you, your spell on them is broken. The way I see it, I lost my mystique when I began writing this manuscript. I'm now too much of an open book. If you've lost interest in me after four chapters, imagine how I feel after seven plus decades of being me.

2. A week after I was hired at Burnett, the head honcho put his arm around me and said, "Son, you're going to be as big in advertising as you ever dreamt of being in music." He was wrong. The lesson here? Never trust what others say about you. They may have you pegged wrong. But if it turns out they're right, don't let it go to your head.

5

I developed a new school system for boys.
(How to reach the unreachable and teach the unteachable.)

I'M A BOY LIKE TENS of millions of other boys, past and present.

We all hate school with a passion. We have little interest in learning, less interest in books, and no interest in homework. And why should we?

School is boring.

If you don't believe me, you're either a stuffy educator looking to lengthen the school day. A horrid teacher hoping to assign more homework to stressed-out kids.

Or you're a girl.

Girls love school. That's because girls are perfect little creatures. I've known that since nursery school.

But boys? Well, boys will be boys, except for the handful that like school. They're the eggheads, bookworms, and kids who suck at sports. Those brainy children are to be admired. They're the ones who will grow up and make all the scientific and medical breakthroughs we depend on.

But I'll always have a soft spot for the little boy who once blurted out "The End," after his teacher asked him what his favorite part of *20,000 Leagues Under the Sea* was.

I understand that kid.

He was me.

And I am you—the clerk at the local hardware store.

The Uber driver taking passengers to the airport.

And the middle manager sitting behind his desk at a screw manufacturing plant.

I stand in support of all the bored boys who stared out windows and daydreamed while the teacher droned on and on.

"Ricky, can you tell us why General Sherman marched to the blah blah blah?"

"Sorry, Mrs. Cornwall, I wasn't listening."

As one of those kids, I'm uniquely qualified to write about them. My failures in school enable me to look back and examine where my education went wrong. Little of what my teachers taught caught my interest, fostered a love of learning, or ignited a curiosity inside of me.

I was passionless.

Maybe I have no right to complain, though. By the time I finished five years of college and two summer school sessions, I wound up with a solid eighth-grade education.

To this day I can't quote Shakespeare. Can't recite poetry. Can't speak any foreign languages. Nor can I do Thursday, Friday, Saturday or Sunday crossword puzzles. And I'm unsure about the use of commas, so I insert them by utilizing a little comma sense. Now why do you think that is?

It's not because my teachers were all dreadful.

Or because my parents didn't push me to excel.

Or because I spent way too much time in class after school.

I will not stare at Nancy again… I will not stare at Nancy again…

No. It was because I wasn't engaged in the curriculum.

Before you jump to the conclusion that I'm moronic, I'd like to write that I have nothing against math, science and history. I'm all for reading and writing. And I firmly believe art and music play a crucial role in education. But I do take exception to the way the school system teaches those subjects. They take what should be enjoyable—learning—and turn it into pure drudgery.

Don't school boards realize that boys en masse aren't capable of doing good work. They're too immature to accomplish anything of quality.

Ask them to trim hedges and I'll promise you an uneven row.

Tell them to lay bricks and I'll show you a lopsided house.

At eleven, I delivered newspapers to more bushes than houses.

But ask boys to play a game and watch them explode with joy. They'll play their hearts out and perform far beyond classroom expectations. I don't have to guess what most boys' favorite subjects are in school.

They're recess and gym.

Rather than force-feeding facts and numbers to these boys in a traditional sense, why not teach to their love of sports instead. To their love of competition. Or to put it another way, why not make learning fun?

Compelling fun. Imaginative fun. Captivating fun.

I want to have more fun.

Or as Mary Poppins once sang:

"A spoonful of sugar helps the medicine go down."

That means it's time to light a fire under all the bored boys of America through their own starry-eyed dreams of hitting homers, running for touchdowns, and hitting game-winning threes.

If you're a prickly educator, you might find this idea crazy. But before you go running to the principal's office, know this. Most everything taught in a traditional classroom setting can be taught just as well through the prism of sports.

For instance, there's math in statistics, science in the physiology of athletes, and history in the creation of games and leagues.

There's physics in the angular momentum of a home run, social studies in player unions, and reading in sports biographies.

And there's writing in sports reporting, public speaking in sports announcing, and business in sports endorsements.

These are just a few examples of how sports can teach academic subjects without dulling kids' senses. And the list of potential subject matter goes on and on. It's a liberating, self-pedagogical approach to learning—and to developing necessary critical thinking skills.

But don't be surprised that once these educational seeds are all planted, these same kids will grow intellectually and discover that their curiosity leads to other interests.

If my school had taught academic subjects through an all-encompassing sports program, I would have read every book, written every paper, done every homework assignment, and studied for every test. I can only wonder what I might have been if I had gone to *Sports School?*

An astrophysicist sounds good to me.

I always had my head in the clouds anyway.

While on the topic of physics, I once watched Nobel Laureate Leon Lederman teach science to an inner-city second-grade classroom. He blew giant bubbles and had the kids come up and pop them. It was wonderfully involving. But the kicker was when he posed a simple child-like question to the class.

"Why do bubbles burst when you touch them?"[1]

It inspired the children, boys and girls alike, to think. Watching them made me jealous of all the cool stuff I missed out on.

Too bad we don't have more "Leon Ledermans" around to inspire classrooms. But seeing that we don't—and never will—we either have to endure the ramifications of a society with millions of undereducated boys.

Or give school systems a mandate to change the way bored boys are taught.

I'll vote for *Sports School* every time. It's the universal language of boys. Most coaches and gym teachers already know this. They've been saying for years that sports are life's best teachers. Yet school administrators have refused to listen, calling them a bunch of dumb jocks.

Why don't you try saying that to Ryan Fitzpatrick's face.[2]

I promise, if I'm ever named Secretary of Education, boys will be smarter—and a whole lot happier.

And that will make me happy too. Unless it depresses me first.

---

1. When you touch a bubble, it pops because your finger is drier than the moisture inside the bubble. That causes the bubble's outer skin to evaporate until it grows thinner and thinner—and *pops!* But don't bat an eyelash or you'll miss it.

2. Ryan Fitzpatrick, former New York Jets quarterback, attended Harvard and scored a 1580 on his SAT's.

6

I'm the happiest depressed guy you'll ever meet.
(How to live with depression and wake up smiling.)

I WOULD HAVE COMMITTED suicide yesterday. If I hadn't been curious about how my life would turn out today.

I'm happy I waited.

This morning, I drove to my local coffee haunt and chatted with friends before proceeding to the library to write. Among the old and dusty stacks of books, I got lost in times past and became young again.

Then I ate a delicious lobster roll for lunch—*mmm*—and sipped a Diet Coke—*ahh*—and thanked God I was alive. On my ride home, I sang along to the cheerful tunes on my car radio and let out a contented belch.

Later, my wife and I went out for dinner with my sister and brother-in-law. We talked, laughed and overate. Then I went home, watched some TV, and texted two of my kids to make sure they were safe. When they texted back, I sighed in relief.

At night's end, as I lay in bed reviewing my life, like many men are prone to do in the dark, my last thought was to hang myself. But I never could have gone through with it.

I didn't own a rope.

The next day I again walked around with a big grin on my face, the result of a pretty young woman half my age smiling in my direction. But as my head hit the pillow that evening, I realized she was just humoring an old man. I felt like sticking a gun in my mouth. But I never could've pulled the trigger.

I wanted to see how much I'd weigh in the morning.

By dawn, a couple of disappearing pounds saved my sorry ass. I thought isn't life grand? And I resolved to never buy a gun.

There's nothing better in life than to look forward to the next day.

Next days embrace hopeful promise.

I met my wife the next day.

Next days present us with a future better than the present.

I got the job I wanted the next day.

Next days keep me happy and alive.

I watched the Cubs win the World Series the next day.

Many wondrous things happen on next days, even if the law of averages says otherwise. So why should you shoot your entire future to hell because life has fucked you over. Don't you know something spectacular might take place tomorrow that could turn your life around?

It could be a drug that extends life by ten years.

Or a pill that makes assisted suicide a breeze.

Or maybe, just maybe, you're only a day away from meeting the love of your life, getting a big promotion at work, or finding the iPhone you thought you had lost.

Isn't it better to stay alive today? If only for tomorrow's possibilities?

Open your eyes, peeps. Something might cause your pupils to dilate in delight a few minutes from now. It could be a hummingbird hanging in mid-air an arm's length away. Did you know its wings flutter so fast that it clicks like a cricket's chirp?

I'm happy I lived to see it—and hear it.

The thrill may last just a minute, perhaps until a car runs a red light and slams into me at the next intersection.

But dying *unexpectedly* isn't a bad way to go.

It's just a quick cut to black. The same as it was for Tony in the *Soprano's* iconic last episode. But on the offhand chance I survive, I had a living will with a resuscitation order drawn up years ago.

Say I make a miraculous recovery from something that should've killed me but leaves me a paraplegic. Isn't life still worthwhile if I can snack on a bag of Oreos the next day?

Or smack my lips on buttered bread?

Or chow down on a sausage pizza with no concern of weight gain, diabetes or heart disease?

It's like becoming a teenager all over again.

But one thing I won't do, regardless of how long I live, is order another corned beef sandwich on rye. Twenty-five years ago, I bit into my first one since my early twenties. I thought it would make my life more fulfilling. But it just made me want to floss. Certainly no reason to kill one's self, but who wants to live forever anyway?

I know I don't.

Then again, it must be boring as hell doing absolutely nothing for a deathtime, (the opposite of a lifetime). Because there are no next days for dead people.

Except for the ones who come back to life after they're gone—(only Jesus and Frankenstein's monster as of this writing).

I'm pretty sure I want to live at least one more day when I think of doing myself in. As I say to friends, I'm addicted to oxygen. I love it more than life itself. I want to live for tomorrow's air, unmindful that the air quality may not be as good as it is today.

Oddly enough, I'm not afraid to die. It can't be any worse than having never been born. But if I have my druthers, I'll take a little *somethingness* over a future of *nothingness* any day.

Tomorrow's something doesn't have to be huge either. Like I tell my children, I don't have to win the Powerball lottery to make myself happy. The evidence in support of that is I seldom play the lottery. If I won, I'd still lose. I'd squander my identity. I'd no longer be the *Poor Rick* I was in the autobiographical song I wrote over fifty years ago.

> *Poor Rick*
> *Couldn't explain*
> *Why he sat and stared*
> *Poor Rick*
> *Was going nowhere*
> *He lived in a dream*
> *Though real it seemed*
> *He knew it would fly away*

I'd be Rich Rick instead.

Hell, I prefer to stay right where I am. Living in the sometimes *happier* here and the sometimes *sadder* now. Call me crazy if you must, but I'm comforted when I'm brooding, saddened when I'm pleased. It's an excellent position to be in.

I'm living proof that depression and happiness can co-exist. You'd never guess I wasn't up on the days I'm down. I show no outward signs of despair.[1] My shoulders aren't slumped, the furrows in my forehead run shallow, and my crow's feet can only be defined as Santa Claus crinkly.

Gee, maybe Santa suffers from the same condition I do?

But neither do I wish to convey that I'm bi-polar—a Dr. Jekyll and Mr. Hyde type character. Good-hearted one moment, evil the next.

That said, I'd be misleading you if I didn't acknowledge some of the stupid, hurtful things I've done in the past.

Like the night I faked a heart attack in front of my ten-year-old son Scott.[2]

Or the day I cow-licked my daughter Alison's face.

Or the time I let my saliva drip into my son Jamie's open mouth.

Those are just three parental guilt stories of mine. I've got plenty of others.

Rather than listing them all here, I'll just type that I'll be happier if they one day forgive me and sadder if they don't. Either way, my thoughtless actions have scarred me for life.[3]

As a consequence, I'm ready for any future punishments I may have coming.

Preferably tomorrow.

Meanwhile, film rights to my story are available today.

---

1. When I'm depressed, I grind my teeth. But only my dentist can tell that my teeth have shortened in recent years. I'm not exaggerating when I write I've redefined what growing old is all about. I can truthfully say I'm not long in tooth.

2. My son Scott sat lovingly in my arms when I faked my heart attack. The pain I feel in my heart for scaring him—and scarring him—continues to weigh on me. As payback for my sin, I had a well-deserved, real heart attack twenty-eight years later.

3. For many years, I carried the *stigmata*—the markings of the wounds of Christ— on my wrists and ankles. Then one day, around the turn of the Millennium, they disappeared. I haven't suffered a single day since. Only nights.

7

I outsourced a movie to India.
(How to follow through on your crazy ideas.)

I ALWAYS WANTED TO be a filmmaker.

As a writer—*slash*—producer of commercials, news features and documentaries, moviemaking seemed like the next logical step in my daydreaming career. (*See Chapter 12 for details.*)

And not the pipe dream that it is.

But before I had embarked on any of my future careers, I tried writing a couple of TV scripts that were shot down by the powers that be. Much like literary agents and book publishers nixed this book left and right when I submitted it. But that's mainly because most of them wouldn't dare publish anything from an old white guy. Age and the color of my skin has made me invisible to the world.

I'll never give up…I'll never give up. I don't care how old I get, I'll never give up.

I just found a way to work around those dream blockers. That's what you do when door after door closes on you.

My first and only Hollywood opportunity came a few months after I joined the *Today* show. I received a call from Touchstone Pictures about a story Mike Leonard and I had done on kids' art. They compared it to a mini-movie and asked if we might be interested in developing a screenplay.

39

It just so happened we were collaborating on one at the time. It was about my father's exploits in World War II—and the fortune in diamonds he had buried in Japan at war's end.[1] But I had just gotten the TV gig and wasn't about to call it quits so fast. I said nothing to Touchstone about our work-in-progress.

Instead, I said we didn't have time for it.

I wish I hadn't.

But with a wife, three kids, a mortgage, and two car payments, I was too immersed in my present life to embark on another. Yet I never gave up on the dream. Many times I considered going the indie route, but whose money was I going to use? Certainly not my own.

And just like that—*pfft*—the dream was over. Until the day it wasn't.

With the advent of outsourcing, the timing was perfect for a wannabe filmmaker to sneak into Hollywood through the sub-continental backdoor entrance.

Bollywood.

And that's how *The Hindi Indie* was born.

In a clear case of life imitating art, *The Hindi Indie* was about a displaced American call center worker who uncovers the potential evils of foreign call centers and their capacity to blackmail American citizens. He's convinced that the story would make a good movie. But no studio in Hollywood will let him pass through the front door which forces him to go in a different direction.

He outsources the movie to India.

Upon his arrival in to Mumbai, however, he falls prey to Mrs. Sippy (pronounced Mississippi), an unscrupulous Indian producer who secretly pads her profits by implementing stringent cost-cutting measures. Going so far as outsourcing elements of the film to even less expensive third-world countries—and pocketing the difference.

To satisfy her lust for money, she hires a Taliban video store clerk from Afghanistan to write the script, a one-eyed Pakistani cameraman as cinematographer, and an accordion teacher from Mozambique to compose the score. She then kidnaps actor Ron Silver while he's vacationing in India and strongly encourages him to play the lead male role.

She tortures him with sitar music.

Written with apologies to George Harrison.

Once filming commences, the movie quickly turns into a comedy of errors. There's no continuity from scene to scene and the plot makes no sense—leaving our wannabe filmmaker broke, desperate and confused.

But all is saved when the disjointed footage winds up in the hands of a mysterious Buddhist monk. Now in charge of editing this hapless film, the monk finds inspiration from *Mad Magazine* Fold-Ins, in which a serious question is first posed and then humorously answered when the page is folded accordion-style. The monk borrows that same technique to edit what began as a drama into an uproarious, screwball comedy.

The *Hindi Indie* becomes a big international hit.

Once I had outlined the above plot, I emailed the storyline to the top ten Indian studios to gauge their interest in filming it. I got back eight replies. The two most promising ones came from Kunal Dasgupta, the CEO of Sony India. And Prakash Jha, the Martin Scorcese of Indian filmmaking.

To my way of thinking, *The Hindi Indie* was an exercise in mental masturbation—a way to get my rocks off without deserving to get my rocks off. But Indians likened it to a grand social experiment—a chance to show the world that India could make films every bit as entertaining as Hollywood could.

Hooray for Bollywood!

But first I needed a script.

Kunal and Prakash gave me the names of the seven top Indian screenwriters. The one that stuck out was Farrukh Dhondy, a well-respected Indian screenwriter, playwright, and essayist living in England. I contacted him through his London literary agent, Nicky Lund of David Higham Associates.

Farrukh got so excited about the project that he waived his usual upfront fee for a higher percentage on the back end. No way I could pass on a deal like that. I flew to London and started working with Farrukh on the script.

Meanwhile, Kunal from Sony called again to tell me he couldn't start production on my movie for two years due to previous commitments.

"Be patient, Richard," he said.

Two years? I didn't have that kind of time. I might be dead by then. So, I moved Prakash Jha up to the head of the list, even though he was famous for making dramas—and not the comedy that Farrukh would be writing.

But that soon changed when Farrukh introduced me to "The Fatties." Their sobriquet fitted their position as heavyweights in both gluttony and filmmaking. They owned a studio in London and had produced dozens of successful movies in both the UK and India. "The Fatties" bought into the project from the get-go. And brought in Peter Ansorge, the former head of programming for the UK's illustrious Channel Four, to run the production.

Too embarrassed to call Prakash back, I canceled his involvement in an email. And that's when *The Hindi Indie* began to fall apart.

Or maybe it was when Saraswati, the Hindu Goddess of the arts, turned against me.

Real life disasters struck. First, Hollywood B-list actor Ron Silver, who had agreed to play the role of A-list-actor Ron Silver in the film, went AWOL.

He forgot to mention he had esophageal cancer when he accepted the role.

Then a critical location in my film, the Taj Hotel in Mumbai, went kaboom on me.

How was I to know real-life terrorists would attack it?

And who could have foreseen that "The Fatties" would be indicted for tax evasion? The authorities turned off the lights in their shuttered studio, leaving Farrukh and me out in the cold.

The following year I had one last chance to make *The Hindi Indie* when the script fell into the hands of John Landis, the director of *Animal House*. He loved the concept like everyone else had, but said he would never shoot in India again. Called it the most repulsive place on Earth.

Landis said it. I didn't. I love Indians. Both kinds.

That made it nearly impossible for Farrukh to call upon any of his Indian contacts to help fund the production. And without additional Indian money, Landis wouldn't be able to make any movie. Anywhere.

That's because a rotating helicopter blade had decapitated leading man Vic Morrow during the filming of *The Twilight Zone* movie that Landis had directed years earlier. After that miscue, he was persona non grata around Tinseltown. Upon learning that news, I thought it best to walk away from Landis ASAP.

And that's when *The Farsi Farce* was born.

It was just another boy meets girl story. But this time the boy was a girl and the girl was a boy. And the whole thing took place in homophobic Iran.

While being filmed in Mexico.

I'll never give up…I'll never give up. I don't care how old I get; I'll never give up.

As for this book, the jury is still out whether publishers were right to turn it down. But, in the hands of Amazon Publishing who knows? Maybe pipedreams do come true.

Stranger things *have* happened.

---

1. During World War II, my dad was among the first wave of marines to land in Nagasaki after *Fat Man,* the second atomic bomb, had been dropped. In the ruins of the Mitsubishi factory, he stumbled upon a metal lockbox filled with diamonds. Doing what any red-blooded American boy would do in circumstances like that, he stole the box and buried it in a cemetery on a farm on the outskirts of town. Where they likely remain to this day because my dad was too scared to take them home after the war. (It would have been a war crime.) And because he died without telling me the exact location of the damn farm.

8

I grew a plant on my big toe.
(How to grow an unwanted plant—and grow up at the same time.)

IF TRUTH IS INDEED stranger than fiction, then I was once a freak of nature, sharing disfigurement with ridiculed carnival sideshow acts and maligned castoffs from *Ripley's Believe It or Not.*

How else can I explain the shocking condition that befell me during my (event filled) first month of college?

When I first saw the plant growing underneath my toenail, I was pretty sure I might be the only person to suffer from this unusual malady. Rather than brag about it, I thought it best to keep it hidden from my newly-gained, pre-hippie fraternity brothers. I considered that a better choice than incurring the laughter—*haha*—and the cringes—*yuck*—of wider public discovery. Which I'm pretty sure you're doing right now.

Worse yet, if word got out, I was concerned I might become the darling of future farmers in the Agriculture Department.

I like square-dances, hayrides and hoe downs as much as the next guy, but...

Nonetheless, I'm honor-bound to ask what needs to be asked. Is it fair to equate my temporary twist of fate with someone else's permanent physical disfigurement?

Not a chance.

Yet there are similarities between the two. Both can turn a person into a social pariah.

Or, as it relates to long ago college freshmen, the laughingstock of the University of Illinois campus. That is why I didn't share my affliction with anybody—and I mean nobody.

There's no name for the condition I had. (I couldn't find it on the internet as I wrote this.) But if I were still a working adman, I'd call it *Arbordigitoesis*. That pretty much sums up my disorder quite nicely. That's because I was pretty good at coming up with meaningful names for products back when I was—well, meaningful myself.

I came up with "Smile Wipers"—miniature sponges that kids wrapped around their finger to wipe their teeth squeaky clean.

Hey, Billy, my mom never makes me brush my teeth.

And then I dreamt up "S'not"—a lubricant developed for chronic dry nose syndrome.

Nose still dry?—sniff sniff—"S'not!"

And who can forget "Sun Seasons"—hydroponic lettuce grown under ideal conditions by Kraft Foods.

Each leaf perfect, season after season after season.

My big toe was also flawlessly leafy. Three leaves if I remember correctly. Enough to make a small tossed salad.

Well, for a rodent anyway.

Ta-da.

Introducing *Toe Greens* from—you're not going to believe this, but my mother's maiden name was Kraft—yes, the Kraft family of Racine, Wisconsin. The birthplace of this writer.

Maybe if I had come from some underdeveloped country, I might have better understood my affliction. For example, in the Amazon Rainforest, one might expect to see a plant growing out of a toe.

Or a string bean attached to a scalp.

Or a peapod ripening inside a lung.

The internet claims they've all happened before. I have no idea how or why. But I learned from the film *Jurassic Park* that life always finds a way to thrive. In my case, it found its way onto my big toe—a most peculiar place for a plant to grow.

I imagine I could have blamed my frat house for the plant *implanted* under my toenail. During pledge week they had ordered us to go out day and night in torrential downpours.

But it was me who wore wet socks all day.

Me who never dried out his waterlogged shoes by the radiator at night.

Me who traipsed through deep puddles because I was too lazy to walk around them.

By the time I got around to showering at week's end, my big toe had fully blossomed. Even without my contact lenses on, it was tough to miss. Particularly the little white flower that had sprouted up on one of the three tiny branches.

"What the hell is that?" I said to nobody but myself.

I marveled at it for a short while. It was the perfect boutonnière for *The Incredible Shrinking Man,* should he be invited to a formal affair. Then I toweled myself off and sat on the edge of my bed to examine it.

And to contemplate a course of action.

I suppose I could have gone to a podiatrist to have it removed. In retrospect, I should have. It's possible the toenail fungus I now suffer from began with that innocent-looking plant rooted underneath my nail.

Or I could have seen a gardener. He could have treated my toe with weed killer.[1]

One thing I couldn't do, however, was to let my plant just stay there and grow. What if it spread to other parts of my body?

What if I grew hedges on my forehead?

A garden on my chin?

Or a lawn running up my arm?

It would have turned me into the first human Chia.

It left me no choice but to tug it. Twist it. Pull it.

Until the root began to slide out and o-----u-----t and o-------u-------t. All two and a half bloody centimeters of it. (A little over an inch.)

Go on. Laugh and cringe at my expense.

It's a lot easier to do that than to address human abnormalities of any kind. But I don't feel right ending this chapter without acknowledging those with the courage to face much more serious deformities.

Yes, I was a freak of nature once. But only until I threw my "toe plant" in the garbage. A lot of men, women and children have no choice in the matter.

Their toes are forever green.

I didn't used to think about things like that as a young man. But now my life, after tens of thousands of passing hours, has gone and done a flip-flop on me.

Now I care about things I didn't use to care about.

Now I see deep meanings where none existed.

Now I can't write a silly story about my green toe without seeing a still life of the human condition.

Yeah, I once had a green toe. But I've never grown anything else since then.

Except older and wiser.

And maybe a wee bit healthier.

---

1. I now see a podiatrist six times a year to have my toenails cut. No, he doesn't use a hedge trimmer.

9

I found a cheap alternative to costly health insurance.
(How to stick it to the man.)

THE ABOVE CHAPTER HEADING is one hefty claim to make.

Almost as hefty as the claims you make when you get sick, have surgery, or get a sudden attack of the sniffles—all causing premiums and deductibles to skyrocket year after year.

But the thing is, you don't have to sit there and take it. With a little ingenuity, you can fight back. As I did when I searched for a lower cost alternative to traditional healthcare plans. After considerable effort, I found one I could put to the test.

Yes, I was the guinea pig for my own health insurance experiment.

No, I wasn't caged in a laboratory.

But I am acting sort of cagey right now in revealing this alternative health insurance option of mine. That's because I'm about to let you in on a little-known secret.

A secret that could save seniors (the citizen kind, not the student kind) lots of money. Big money. But before I get into what I did—and how I did it—let me first share the cost benefits I accrued from putting my little discovery into practice.

I cut my annual health insurance premiums from $26,200 to $2,025. And sliced my annual deductible from $2,500 to $200. In total, I saved a staggering $70,300 in healthcare costs over three years.[1]

Wondering how I did it?

Easy. I did it by necessity.

When the financial meltdown struck in 2008, it swept away my business—along with my pricey health insurance. Unable to get new coverage due to a litany of preexisting conditions—Type II diabetes, heart disease and arthritis—I became desperate. What I needed was a three-year stopgap measure till I went on Medicare, but nothing was available. I was about to give up the hunt when fate intervened. It turned out that I was staring at the remedy the whole time.

It was my son Jamie.

Home from college for the weekend, we were chatting one evening about who-knows-what when I was struck by a revelation. If Jamie goes to college and gets student health insurance, why can't I?

It turned out I could.

That's right. I went back to college at age sixty-one to get the best low-cost coverage a pre-medicare guy could get.[2]

My wife bragged to her friends that I was majoring in pre-med.

To pull it off, I enrolled as a degree seeking student at Northwestern's School of Continuing Education. But at one-twentieth the cost of regular Northwestern.

This wasn't just night school filled with thirty- and forty-somethings, however. Lots of undergrads unable to fit all their required subjects into their day schedules were in my classes too. They found my solution to health insurance hilarious.

As did thousands of other students around the country when my son posted "my little secret" on Reddit's *Ask Me Anything* section. It became the number one post within an hour.

Yep, old man me had gone viral.

My lighthearted AMA answers were infectious.

It goes without saying that a few sourpusses bawled me out. They'd write stuff like, "You're gaming a system not meant for old uninsurable guys."

But healthcare is nothing to fool around with. So I made sure everything was on the up and up before I applied to Northwestern. My first step was to call the Student affairs office to make sure I was eligible for student insurance if I enrolled.

"No issue," they said.

But to make sure everything was absolutely kosher, they suggested I double-check with their insurance carrier.

"No issue," they said.

So off to classes I went. Free of guilt. Free of high deductibles. And free of expensive premiums. But the best part was that I had managed to put myself into a younger, and therefore healthier, insurance pool. It lowered costs significantly.

Geez, when I put it that way, it does sound like I gamed the system.

But my orthopedic surgeon, endocrinologist, ophthalmologist and cardiologist all believed otherwise. They all agreed I had come up with an ingenious solution. My primary physician even went so far as to say I had solved the national healthcare crisis, later recommending my solution to other patients in the same sinking boat I was in.

But here's the kicker, (as if saving seventy thousand dollars wasn't enough reason to go to college). It turned out I only had to take two classes a year to maintain my full-time student status. I signed up for both courses during the fall trimester, and followed up with a leave of absence during the winter and spring trimesters.

In all, I took six classes over three years, totaling up to fourteen thousand dollars for tuition, books and insurance.

Plus, I enjoyed a few other neat benefits while attending. I got six A's, ended up on the Dean's list three times, and studied and flirted with pretty coeds—if coeds even exist anymore. Oh, and before I forget, I was asked to join a fraternity.

As a married student, I chose to live in my dorm room at home.

And get this. I did it all while maintaining my class clown status from childhood.

Not one professor had the nerve to send me out to the hall.

After finishing up at NU, forty years after graduating from the University of Illinois, I finally learned I was smart enough to be whatever I wanted to be.[3]

Good thing I didn't become an actuarial scientist, though. I wouldn't want to know when I was going to die. But because of *me* being the guy I turned out to be, I discovered the wonders of Adderall and signed up for a humanities class that led me to professional storytelling.

And ultimately, to the writing of this book.

Let that be a lesson for every last one of you. Every action you take begets another. So if you want to know what lies ahead in your future, get moving now.

Unless you're an old codger like me and have little future left.

As for my healthcare solution, I have no idea whether it will still work today. They may have changed the rules now that I've been outed.

But if you're a pre-Medicare senior and need a great low-cost coverage plan, it's worth a call to see if you can sign up for "RicKare" at your nearby university today. Be sure to mention my name.

Or maybe not.

With my reputation, it could lead to a vicious fight.

---

1. My insurance costs were in 2009 dollars. Today, the savings would be far greater.

2. Since I was over sixty when I enrolled at Northwestern, I didn't need to take a physical to qualify for student health insurance. If I had been a year younger, the school and the insurer might have rejected my request for coverage due to preexisting conditions.

3. I fell in love with astrophysics during my three trimesters at Northwestern. For the first time, I realized what you see isn't necessarily what you get. That hypothesis applies as much to a single atom as it does to the entire universe. Or it will apply to that as soon as someone proves the Grand Unified Theory. It ain't gonna be me, though.

10

I saw Mike Tyson kick down a steel door.
(How to live a normal life when you're anything but normal.)

MIKE TYSON WAS A terrifying guy, an athletic freak of nature with sinewy muscles compressed into a package of brute strength.

But you probably know that.

In the ring, he was a caged beast stalking his prey, scaring the bejesus[1] out of anybody standing in his way.

But again, I'm sure you know that.

When the "baddest man on the planet" fought Michael Spinks for the heavyweight crown back in 1988—a match I covered for NBC Nightly News—the bout was over before it began. Prior to the bell, Tyson stared down the fear-stricken Spinks. Then proceeded to KO him in ninety-one seconds.

But you probably know that too.

So here's something you don't know about the Tyson-Spinks bout. Tyson had fought another vicious fight the previous day and had recorded another ferocious knockout. One that was never publicized. I know this because I was in the room when it happened.

I saw Mike Tyson kick down a heavy-duty steel door, a security exit that looked like a prison entrance to solitary confinement. I was sure he'd break his leg or bust up his knee at the time. But Tyson got the better of the door, kicking it in with his leg raised up like a battering ram out of the Middle Ages.

The only other athlete I ever saw exhibiting anything approximating Tyson's raw power was Bo Jackson. He defied gravity by running horizontally on an outfield wall, leaving baseball fans awestruck. But Tyson's feat was far more impressive. Something akin to Superman's alien superpowers.[2]

Who else but a man of steel could kick down a door of steel, right? Except Tyson didn't do it to save Jimmy or Lois from the clutches of villains. He did it because he was angry with his wife, actress Robin Givens. Evidently, they had argued minutes before Mike had entered the workout room. But nobody present knew that yet.

Ignorant of the conflict brewing between husband and wife, the press sat and watched Tyson put on a display of physical prowess seldom seen in pre-fight workouts. We *oohed* when he jumped rope at three times the speed of mere mortals. And *aahed* as he pummeled the speed bag in a rhythm that kept pace with *The Flight of The Bumblebee*.

And then his wife entered the room.

Tyson's mood changed straightaway. He stalked out the heavy bag while staring at Givens menacingly. He delivered damaging body blows to her—*er, the bag's*—mid-section—*uh, kidneys*.

Tyson was fighting mad, pounding that bag for close to fifteen seconds before storming off to the exit. But instead of opening the door, he picked up steam and—*BAM!*—the door was flattened like Michael Spinks would be the next day.

The room froze like a snapshot taken before anybody's ready, catching mouths agape and eye sockets bulging.

Everyone fell silent in fear of what Tyson might do next. He turned and studied the room, daring anyone to challenge him. I don't know why his eyes settled on mine, only that I've attracted unwanted attention too often in my life to ever make me feel invisible.

I averted my gaze lickety-split before he stalked off. And quickly turned my attention to Ms. Givens whose back was turned to me. I couldn't see the expression on her face, but I'm sure she wasn't a happy camper either. Tyson had put on an animalistic exhibition for her benefit that had quieted every reporter in the room. Who knows what Ms. Givens was thinking then. But it all spoke to the dual gentle/bestial nature of Tyson's personality.

As violent as he could be, he spoke in a soft, almost girlish voice.

But you probably know that.

As uneducated as he was, he was introspective and intelligent.

But again, I'm sure you know that.

And as illiterate as he appeared, he quoted poetry and studied philosophy.

But you probably know that too.

So here's something you don't know about the Tyson-Givens fight. Before Tyson entered the ring the following evening, he leaned over and gave Givens—sitting ringside—a sweet little kiss like any apologetic husband would do after a spat. She was sitting in the first row; I was watching from the eighth.

That tender moment between husband and wife ran counter to all the presumptions you might have about Tyson—and the seedy world he came from and presently lived in. I'm sure he would have loved a normal life, but it was unlikely he'd get one. The man was caught in a sphere of influence that stood in direct opposition to customary living.

I witnessed it all firsthand.

At the Tyson-Spinks fight, I was introduced to a world that I had assumed only existed in movies.

I saw hoodlums wearing pinkie rings and packing heat.

Platinum blonde gun molls with *Betty Boop* Bronx accents.

And high society sophisticates smoking cigarettes in fancy holders.

I wanted no part of this circle. It made me feel mentally imbalanced. And I couldn't help but think that Tyson felt the same way before he leaned over to kiss his wife.[3]

But no tender moment could save the man.

As for me, the lesson I learned at the Tyson-Spinks fight was nothing unusual. I discovered that I love an ordinary life.

In spite of any grand illusions, I might have.

But who needs to live in a fantasy world when creative non-fiction seems to seek you out in the real world?

---

1. Do Jews get the *bemoses* scared out of them?

2. Unlike real aliens, Superman doesn't exist. He was the brainchild of Jerry Siegel and Jerry Shuster. He was initially given the means to propel himself faster than a speeding bullet, not by flying, but by taking super-leaps into the air using his super-strong leg muscles. Since Superman had no anti-gravitational powers back in the 1930's, he had no way of increasing his speed in flight. As his momentum diminished, he would often fall from the sky—a dead giveaway that Superman was a man of fiction. Even though he's flown with acceleration since the 1940s.

3. Givens divorced Tyson four months later.

11

I don't put more effort into life than I need to.
(How to use laziness to overcome your limitations.)

I COULD START THIS EVALUATION of Rick Leslie by writing about my *fatal flaw*.

Or I could choose to elaborate on my *vital virtue*.

It doesn't matter which one I pick. Because my fatal flaw and my vital virtue are one and the same. Both my curse and my blessing.

Together they turn me into someone worth knowing as much as someone you'd just as soon forget. Someone of accomplishment and someone who fell far short.

I'll let you decide what side I lean to more. But before you choose, you should know how my fatal flaw and vital virtue manifest themselves in the *plus-minus* column of human nature. That being this:

I'm lazy.

So lazy that *old* me can't wait to finish this book, do the rewrite, correct the grammar, and fix the typos.

I want to get back to my old life of TV, couches and carryout.

So lazy that young *me* was summed up this way on his third-grade report card.

"Ricky is lazy. He does not take his homework seriously and makes little effort to improve himself."

Miss Cornwall sure had me pegged right. I seldom did the best I could. I was a born minimalist, doing just enough to get by while never putting out the energy to excel at anything.

And that, of course, reduced my chances of ever becoming a runaway success.

That. And a little of this:

It's damn near impossible to move to the top of the A-list when you don't utilize all the tools you have, and you ignore all the hard work success demands.

Especially when you're competing against superstars.[1]

That's just one of the many, many debits I've racked up in my minus column.

With a track record like mine—I once left a job a job at Sears after forty-five minutes—you'd figure I would have fallen flat on my face as a grownup. But I didn't.

That belongs in my plus column.

The reason why was because I was good at what I did. Some would say quite good.

But I was way too lazy to achieve stardom. The time I would have spent trying to reach the pinnacle of success would have greatly reduced the time I needed just to get someone to notice me in the first place.[2]

Ironically, my laziness led to a competitive edge in the marketplace. Not being good enough to be the star of the show helped me become good enough to succeed as a solid supporting act.

Hey, Paul Schaffer did quite well standing next to David Letterman, didn't he?

It turned out that all of my daydreaming—the first love of lazy people everywhere—wasn't a time-waster after all. The effort I put into reverie went to far better use than the time I put into self-improvement.

Yep. Old-fashioned daydreaming was the incubator and curator of my best ideas. Without it, I would have been nothing.

Not even a truck driver as my brother-in-law once said.

For the benefit of Miss Cornwall who, if alive, might be interested in knowing how *Lazy Rick* turned out, I provide further examples two through five.

Two: Thanks to laziness, I followed the path of least resistance. The most straightforward solution always took precedence.

What other way could I have doubled the raise I got from my boss?

Three: Thanks to laziness, I discovered shortcuts in problem-solving that helped me work faster and with greater efficiency.

How else could I have beaten Simon at his own game?

Four: Thanks to laziness, I generated new strategies for success, often breaking the rules to help me get what I couldn't have gotten any other way.

Otherwise, I never could have made people laugh without saying or doing anything funny?

Five: Thanks to laziness, I compensated for many of my shortcomings by learning to do more with less.

If not for sloth, I would've taken guitar lessons by the book, instead of developing my own original style.

Today, I liken myself to an ex-ballplayer, good enough to have played in the major leagues, even though I never batted more than .250.[3]

How can anyone see that as a minus?

Maybe superstars would. But like I wrote in my prologue, I'm no superstar.

I'm just a guy.

With a vivid imagination.

---

1. At Leo Burnett, I worked alongside future screenwriter and film director John Hughes. He was so good at advertising that I never could have outperformed the guy. I just wasn't as good a writer as he was. (Fewer smarts, lesser talents.) Yet I was good enough to get a job at the same place he did. And bad enough to get fired there too. Oh, well.

2. I also worked alongside one of the top women in advertising—first name, Charlotte. She was the CEO at one of the major agencies I was employed at. Titles notwithstanding, she couldn't tell a good ad from a bad one. In spite of that, Bush 43 named her his Undersecretary of State to help reverse negative Muslim sentiments against America. Pejoratively writing, I never could have done the job she did.

3. Another top advertising executive used the above baseball-hitting analogy when he told me I was on the brink of being sent down to the minors. But this guy couldn't judge a fly ball from an ad campaign. After I smashed five consecutive "metaphoric" home runs, he had to reconsider my demotion and start thinking about his own. He was fired when the agency discovered he was making all his decisions by tossing three Chinese coins on a desk. Evidently, *i Ching*—derived from the ancient Chinese *Book of Changes*—doesn't work well as a decision-making tool for advertising. Or, for that matter, baseball.

12

I'm a professional daydreamer.
(How to live life on your own terms.)

YOU'VE PROBABLY NEVER heard of such a thing before.

It's not like professional daydreaming is listed on any websites or reference books as a career path. And there's no way to major in it in college. Without flunking out, that is.

Which I may or may not have done. Twice.

Yet I became a professional daydreamer.

Daydreaming was the common denominator of every field I've worked in: songwriting, jingle singing, advertising, network news, TV production, and storytelling. How lucky can a guy be to spend his whole professional life doing what he was born to do?

And get paid for it, no less.

Yet professional daydreaming did come at a personal cost.

Though it's the best idea-generating tool ever created, it altered my sense of being. And that's why, even with eyes wide open, I don't always take proper notice of the world around me. I miss things here and there.[1]

That makes me a poor witness if I see a crime being committed.

Detective, are you sure I was held up at gunpoint?

A lousy pick for a bomb-maker.

Which way do the clock hands go? To the left or the right?

And a horrible candidate for "The Good Listener Award."

Sorry. Did you say I was a good whistler?

Maybe that's why regular people can't grasp what a professional daydreamer does. They can't even begin to imagine what it means. They only understand the tried and true, straight and narrow.

And not the creation of something out of nothing—precisely what a daydreaming pro like me does.

Incidentally, that's what makes paid daydreaming positions so attractive to high schoolers and college students, even if they don't quite get what a professional daydreaming job is.

Nonetheless, these young scholars possess a deep respect for the creative process—the provenance of expert daydreamers—but have little appreciation of the hard work it takes to get the wheels spinning.

I do.

If professional daydreaming sounds like a career path worth following, let me be your guide. But before you begin, you'll need a catalyst that causes you to get lost in deep creative thought.

Which is why I stop at green lights and go through red lights more than I care to admit.

I have little inkling of what that imaginative spark might be for you. Or where it might come from.

But once that artistic portal opens, everyone else's cognitive dissonance will become your sweet harmony.[2] And with a good ten years of practice, you'll be thinking like me. (Perish the thought, accountants say.) But only if you direct your newfound talents toward a worthy goal first.

Like I did when I outsourced a movie to India after Hollywood turned me away.

Or when I retaliated against someone who mistreated me by tricking them into paying my office rent.

Or when I penned the shortest poem ever called *The Stammerer.*

I

I

With each of the above examples, I had a major objective in mind. That's the only rule for highly skilled daydreamers. Dream big or don't dream at all.

It just might come true.

Or to paraphrase deceased ad maven Leo Burnett:

"If you reach for the stars, you may not catch one. But you won't end up with a handful of mud either."

I wasn't reaching for much of anything during my senior year of college. Close friends knew I daydreamed a lot, but my daydreams were all leading nowhere. And so was I. Without a purpose to guide me, I had no future.

Then came my lucky break—a professional daydreaming catalyst that I never saw coming. It altered my thinking process forever, and it's ultimately why I'm able to write a memoir/self-help book at all.

I became a well-compensated daydreamer because some girl dumped me.

You read that right. Some heart-breaking little girl left me and, in the process, inadvertently greased the wheels that spun me into action. She was my first love and first hurt. Her rejection was responsible for everything that's happened to me since college.

The pain she caused led to my reinvention.

Let me take you through that fateful day by utilizing the language of algorithms. I like algorithms. They make life simple. All the blanks are filled in for you.

Girl Dumps boy.
Boy is distraught.
Boy picks up roommate's guitar.
Boy can't play guitar.
Boy presses fingers down on fretboard.
Boy plucks strings.
Boy discovers chord by accident.
Then another.
And another.
Boy gets lost in sound.
Time stops.
Chords begin to flow.
A melody pops into boy's head.
Nonsensical words float into boy's mind.
Boy sings over and over.
Words soon take on meaning.
Boy sings about the devastation of loss.
Music makes boy happy.
Boy sees sunrise.
Boy walks to campus.
Boy meets new girl.

I don't know why I picked up the guitar that night, it was the furthest thing from my mind. But the *Candle Song* turned out to be the first song I wrote—voice, instrument, and lyrics all melded into one. In subsequent years, I coined the phrase "song painting" to describe how I wrote my material.

It was the beginning of my daydreaming profession. Against all odds, I had discovered a hidden talent lying within myself.

Maybe a fortuitous life-changing event like that can happen to you. Let's hope it doesn't involve loss of life, limb or income.

But if you're lucky enough to experience love lost, please don't let it go to waste. Always use emotional suffering for your betterment.[3]

I give thanks to the girl who dumped me. She was my first *accidental mentor,* forever unaware of what she had done. By rejecting me, she had opened up a new bandwidth of possibilities for me in the years that followed.

Some people might say she opened up a can of worms.

I learned how to communicate differently.

I learned how to think differently.

And I discovered a God I never believed in.

---

1. As a diehard New York Yankee fan, I loved all things Yankees as a kid—i.e., the stadium, Mantle, Berra, Gillette razors, etc. So you can imagine the agony I went through when I missed the film *Damn Yankees.* It was released weeks before the World Series in 1958. But for some unknown reason, I thought the movie was about the Civil War. By the time I discovered the truth, Mantle had retired and I no longer cared about the Yanks. As for the Civil War, the North went on to become world champions.

2. Professional daydreamers use cognitive dissonance as a way to communicate unforgettable messages. It's achieved by dividing a message into two separate components. Each one is co-dependent on the other but seemingly lying in direct contradiction. The momentary confusion it creates sends the brain into a brief flurry of misfired synapses until the viewer or reader resolves that dissonance—usually in less time than a heartbeat. It's that forced involvement that makes movies, ads and stories memorable. The film title *Mr. Mom* is an example of cognitive dissonance. So is this print ad headline for a new, twin-bin washing machine. *I was the happiest woman alive the day I separated.* And so is a *professional daydreamer.*

3. Physical pain can be used to your benefit as much as emotional pain. By way of illustration, I quit smoking after knee replacement surgery in 1996. My surgical pain made it easy to stop. Tobacco was the furthest thing from my mind during my hospital stay. I went four whole days without craving a cigarette. By the time I got home, I had kicked the habit for good. That's how effective pain can be as a motivating force in your life.

13

I found God at Northwestern University.
(How to become a believer in miracles when miracles don't exist.)

I NEVER BELIEVED IN God. Until I took two classes at Northwestern University.[1]

Astrophysics and evolution.

Those two classes led me to a God I had never found during all the hours I spent at Sunday school, Hebrew school, funerals, weddings, bar mitzvahs and Seders. Which, as things go, way overestimates the number of actual hours I spent in service to Jews because I avoided most religious observances after I turned eleven.

But today I'm a true believer. I know it defies logic to introduce God into your life these days, but who—other than Einstein—would have believed time was a variable back in 1904?[2]

Get my drift…You, atheist, you?

To put it bluntly, what you see isn't necessarily what you get.

In both science *and* religion.

If you're a true believer in God the old-fashioned religious way, you might want to keep this chapter in your hip pocket when somebody calls you an ignorant dumbass.

I suspect many readers, mainly those with half a brain, might also call me nuts for accepting the existence of God at such a late stage in my life. They might even believe I found God just because I'm a septuagenarian, hence closing in on death with every word I type. It's okay if you believe that. Just don't call me stupid, though. It's not like everyone who believes in *It* is an ignorant Republican hick farmer.

It just happens to be a minority position I happen to hold.

Fact is, research studies show only 3.3 percent of brainy people believe in God. I'd like to think I fall somewhere within that category, but I can't be sure, given that I have no idea how smart or dumb I might be.

Truthfully, I might be both at the same time.

All I know for sure is that the *God Flock* never included evolutionary biologists Steven Jay Gould and Richard Dawkins. Both smart men. Both atheists. And both believers in natural selection.

I believe in it too. (I've seen no evidence to the contrary.) But I'm not one hundred percent sure Darwin got evolution a hundred percent right. After all, one of his findings in *The Descent of Man* was that females and people of color were of inferior intelligence. I suspect Mr. Darwin may have been swayed by the times, if not by insufficient data. Those were the days when learned men didn't always reason correctly.

Now everybody ignores the facts altogether.

However, in their pursuits of science, Hawking and Dawkins always let the facts be their guide, whether they lay Earthbound or heaven sent. So not too surprisingly, both men have accepted the widely held belief among astrophysicists that the universe is filled with intelligent aliens.

On that point, I wholeheartedly agree. But where we split is my belief that smart aliens can't exist within the present framework of the "laws of natural selection" without the existence of a god.

My two classes in astrophysics and natural selection convinced me of that.

What was it about those two subjects that led me to a higher power? Or, more accurately put—a higher *exponential* power?

Ooo, did I just introduce a touch of mystery to this chapter?

It was because I took both courses back-to-back, one right after the other. So when my astrophysics professor said something in class that clashed with something my evolution professor had lectured on an hour earlier, I tried to reconcile the conflict. When I couldn't, it caused me to gasp aloud.

"Oh, my God."

Not in any sense of religious enlightenment.

I had only believed in the Easter Bunny before then.

But because those two courses, when studied together, killed off any chance of intelligent life existing anywhere else in the universe.

And that is what led me to God.

Or was it the other way around? Did God send me to NU to have an epiphany?

These days you can't be too sure of what causes what. And that's what this long, convoluted chapter is really all about. So let me simplify things a bit.

Richard Dawkins refers to natural selection as "blind, unconscious and automatic." It has no goal in mind. Nor does it care if an organism becomes smarter or stronger. Its sole purpose is to help organisms adapt to their present circumstances (habitat) for survival's sake alone.

Could that be why the McRib disappeared from the face of the Earth?

Stephen Jay Gould went one step further than Dawkins when he described evolution this way.

"Wind back the tape of life to the early days of the Burgess Shale;[3] let it play again from an identical starting point, and the chance becomes vanishingly small that anything like human intelligence would grace the replay."

If Gould and Dawkins are both right—and there is no reason to doubt them—human beings had to beat near-infinitesimal odds to have evolved on Earth.

And that creates a paradox.

Because if intelligent life had to beat infinitesimal odds here on Earth, it also would have had to overcome those same overwhelming odds for alien civilizations to exist in galaxies far, far away.

That's because natural selection is an absolute law of nature. By definition, it has to apply across the whole universe as much as it does to Earth. I'm not making that fact up. Both Newton and Einstein proved it. They verified that all planets operate under the same laws of chemistry and physics as Earth does, DNA included.

But that alone doesn't make intelligent life virtually impossible to exist throughout the cosmos.

What follows does.

Though you might assume it's a fifty-fifty chance that a mutation will benefit our genome—it either does, or it doesn't—the reality is much different. The odds of any variant advancing humankind are considered to be less than ten percent.

For higher intelligence to evolve from scratch like it did for us humans, each of the twenty-five thousand beneficial genes in our genome had to line up in perfect sequential order. A few slip-ups along the way and we could have wound up a rodent.

For lovers of Mighty Mouse, that's mighty good news. For mankind—eh—not so good.

So just how great are the odds against intelligent aliens forming elsewhere? I'm no mathematician, but I did study probability theory when I went to college the first time around. The odds of twenty-five thousand genes, each with a ten percent chance of furthering a species, lining up in perfect sequential order is expressed this way.

$$\frac{1}{10}^{25,000} = \text{Human Being} = \text{Human-Like Intelligence Elsewhere}$$

Don't even bother to solve it. The resulting fraction is so small that it makes human beings virtually impossible to exist on Earth.

Yet here we are.

But what about on all those other planets out there spinning round? Each faces the same challenges we face on our planet. Even with the *seven* septillion stars that NASA estimates are out there—more stars than there are grains of sand on Earth—there will never be enough planets in the universe to increase the probability of alien species attaining human-like intelligence through evolution.

The math doesn't lie.

Yet I refuse to accept that answer. For two reasons. First, it's depressing to think we're alone in the universe—nothing more than a random accident that won't happen again in a jillion year.

And second, it doesn't make any sense.

Why would a whole universe void of all thought other than our own even exist?

Worse yet, without a universe, trees can't fall in forests and make sounds.

That question makes me believe the universe is unquestionably teeming with life. But if evolution is blind like Richard Dawkins says it is—here, there and everywhere—then there's no way for alien life to evolve into higher life forms no matter how many billions or trillions of years go by.[4]

Unless—and this is a big *unless.* Unless some yet undiscovered force of nature is also playing a role in natural selection, acting on its behalf to guide life to an inevitable intellectual conclusion.[5]

I choose to believe that force of nature is God simply because it's as good of an answer as any right now.

Sometimes I feel like a prophet.

If it turns out I'm right about living, breathing, thinking aliens being out there, God doesn't need science to exist.

Science needs God.

Spread the word.

Or don't let me take any more college classes.

---

1. I was sixty-one years old when I determined that the God, I had never believed in might be real. How ironic that I went to Northwestern solely to get student health insurance but came out something of a faux-scholar.

2. Albert Einstein published his Specific Theory of Relativity in 1905. One year after everyone became aware that a minute wasn't always a minute.

3. Burgess Shale is the fossil of a failed organism from eons ago.

4. I could make a strong case that all creatures are smart, even if they can't match wits with humans. But no other species on Earth has yet to open a beauty shop, a nail salon, a bank, a dry cleaner or a fast-food restaurant. Though I suspect their absence of doing so might be an indication of even higher intelligence than humans.

5. George Lucas tried to rebrand God in his Star Wars movies by calling It The Force. But nobody was fooled by this disguised reference to God. It was just a sly way for Lucas to assert Its existence without turning off the 96.7% of highly intelligent moviegoers wanting nothing to do with It.

14

I was kicked out of college after four days.
(How to manipulate the world to your advantage.)

LIKE SO MANY UNPOPULAR high school boys, I went off to college an innocent young man.

I'm not saying I had never been kissed.

I had.

Once.

By a cute high school girl who I met at a teenage nightclub called "The Anchor" in downtown Highland Park, Illinois.

Just thinking about that evening reminds me that I was far from kissing material in high school. To be frank, I wouldn't have kissed myself either if I had been a hot girl.

But she was too drunk to know that.

She found an unlocked car and pulled me into the back seat. To my amazement, she started to make out with me. It was my first deep, warm, and lasting kiss ever.

More likely than not, it would have changed my life forever if she hadn't vomited three seconds after her tongue slid down my throat. Thankfully, she withdrew it and spun around first. Or I would have sworn off kissing—and alcohol—forever.

Anyone care for a chucked-up Margarita?

But it was no spoiled kiss that kept me innocent when I went off to college. It was the fact that I was oblivious to the obvious at eighteen. That's what I mean by innocent.

So when I was fixed up with Judy Chinn on my third day at the University of Illinois, I didn't grasp the indisputable fact that I was going out with a Chinese girl. The correlation between the last name *Chinn* and *Chinese* never occurred to me.

Duh.

But I quickly turned a blind eye to my blind date's ethnicity when she walked down the stairs to greet me. I may have had a stunned expression on my face, but it wasn't due to her race.

It was because of her appearance. She was that good looking.

But what does Judy Chinn have to do with virginal Rick—*double chin*—Leslie being kicked out of college?

Everything.

It was all Judy's fault, indirectly writing.

If not for Judy Chinn, I never would have gone out that night.

If not for Judy Chinn, I wouldn't have been anywhere near her dorm when five thousand, sex-starved college boys came screaming for panties.

And if not for Judy Chinn, I wouldn't have looked as guilty as I did after dropping her off that evening, standing on the front stoop of her dorm, seemingly leading the charge, with a coed's undergarment parachuting down atop my head.

It was my first whiff of the female sex organ. Excluding the time my babysitter sat on my face.

But I swear I was innocent.

No, I was naive.

Innocent!

75

I said naive!

Okay. I confess. I was both.

The surging throng had pushed up against me, causing me to lose my balance and fall into a chain-linked handrail. It easily snapped in two and I toppled over, back first.

Right into a large trash bin that upended, spewing garbage all about. Before I could right myself, I was collared by the campus police and had my student ID confiscated.

The next day I received a notice informing me I had been expelled from college for inciting a riot. Ousted on my fourth day of school. Two days before classes had even begun.

How dare they do this to an innocent young man.

My parents would have killed me if they hadn't died before I ever got around to telling them. But there was no need to do so, as the story goes. That's because the university handed me an out-clause.

Apparently, I was able to petition the College Board of Deans for re-admittance if extenuating circumstances were involved.[1]

Extenuating circumstances? Hmm.

I would one day become a master of extenuating circumstances. Always employing this last-gasp effort to escape trouble.

But this was the first time in my life that I had to fend for myself. I wish I could say I was like old TV lawyer Perry Mason—eloquently stating my case, getting all the charges dropped, and having my arrest expunged from my transcript. But I was socially awkward back in 1966 and remain so to this day in many instances.

I can't do tongue twisters at parties because I'm often tongue-tied in the company of other men.

Though no hard evidence was leveled against me, it was evident I was both innocent—(in a moral sense)—and guilty—(in a legal sense)—at the same time. I had no way out other than to speak the truth. I stood disarmingly contrite before the Deans and came clean.

Except for the part about the X-rated and unlaundered cotton underwear crowning my head. Or as old-time comedian Redd Foxx once said...

"Confucius say panties not best thing in life. Just next thing to it."

I omitted the panties business for good reason. And you know what? It worked. The stuffy men and women on the board assumed they would hear excuses from me. In its place they got the truth. Well, pretty damn close to the truth. Apart from the pantie thing, that is.

But here's the truth about using excuses to get yourself out of trouble. They better be believable, or they could backfire on you. While honesty usually stops people cold by neutralizing the cold hard facts against you.

In later years, I would use the truth as a disarming form of manipulation. It was the most important lesson I learned in college.

I learned it all from Judy Chinn, indirectly writing.

Along with my second deep, warm, and lasting kiss ever.

My first without throw up.

Stars exploded with that kiss, as if Ursa Major and Ursa Minor had collided.

---

1. The University of Illinois had given me a twenty percent chance of graduating based on my application. The school was fairly accurate in their assessment. I dropped out of Illinois midway through my freshman year before the school could flunk me out. I returned the following year but then dropped out a second time during my junior year—again due to failing grades. Then I gave it a third and final try and somehow managed to graduate. It astounds me that all the poor grades I received at Illinois got me into Northwestern University forty-two years later.

15

I pranked two Chicago Bear head coaches.
(How to bring peace to two warring parties.)

When are you going to grow up, Leslie? I say to myself.
It's too late for that, I think.

***

YOU MIGHT NOT EXPECT the old outgoing coach of a professional football team and the new incoming coach to be good friends. Especially when the coach just fired and the coach just hired first meet.

It's more likely neither coach would choose to see, or talk, or have anything to do with the other. Behind closed doors, they might even hate each other's guts.

But what if the doors are wide open?

What if they lead straight into a favorite haunt? A chicken and rib joint near the Chicago Bears practice facility? What if new coach Dave Wannstedt—nicknamed Wanny as in wannabe Hall-of-Famer—walks in with his wife on a Friday evening in late January of 1993? And what if I'm waiting for a table there myself? Then I might have to approach the said coach and say hi, right?

Of course, I would. So I say to Wanny, "I'm looking forward to this season with you at the helm. If we can upgrade the defensive line, we should be in good—"

The conversation comes to an abrupt halt when the hostess runs up and tells Wannstedt his table is ready. It infuriates me that he's seated before I am, though I arrived first.

It means my wait for a table will be longer. But I see no way to fix it. Big shot celebrities always get first dibs. But as luck has it, I'll be putting that extra time to good use. Former Bears coach Mike Ditka has just entered the restaurant with his wife, readying the pub for what appears to be a "Two Bears for The Price of One" special.

Oh, boy, Da Coach and Wanny together. In the same restaurant. At the same time. The word serendipitous comes to mind, though I'm not sure of its meaning at that time.

Since the two coaches have never met, I wonder if I can be of help to them in that department. It's worth the chance, I think. If I succeed, it has friction written all over it. I've always been a lover of friction. In my opinion, it's way more entertaining than fiction. It makes me laugh on the inside to see people squirm when they're caught in uncomfortable and often times embarrassing situations.

The thought of bringing Ditka and Wannstedt together reminds me of all the other times I brought the unlikeliest of people together. Like I did in high school, when my parents had two separate phones on an end table in their bedroom. One for my dad's business, the other a family line. They sat side by side, lying in wait for my parents to go out.

Then I'd call two classmates, one from each phone, say the bubbly cheerleader and the quiet shy guy. And then I'd place the mouthpiece of one phone against the earpiece of the other while sneaky me listened in.

Sometimes the stars aligned perfectly and the intended targets answered their phones simultaneously, leaving both parties confused over who called whom. It was entertainment at its best.

Hello?	
	Hello. Who's this?
Don't you know who you're calling?	
	Huh? I didn't call you.
Then why are you on the phone with me?	
	I could ask you the same question.
You know, your voice sounds familiar…	

On and on it went, with me trying to hold in my laughter as I listened in. I guess that made me an immature troublemaker in high school.

As well as an immature troublemaker over a quarter of a century later—when Ditka took his place in line.

The stars were once again aligned in perfect order.

Though Da former Coach has celebrity status in these parts, there's not a single table available. It appears he's stuck in line for a bit. Which gives me ample time to set up the uncomfortable evening I have in store for the two men. Just thinking about it makes my belly jiggle like jelly.

That provides all the encouragement I need to snake my way through the waiting crowd, until I've cozied up to the unsuspecting Ditka.

"Coach," I say. "I wish you were still leading the Bears. The offense is going to suffer without your leadership."

He thanks me for the kind comment. I rub my hands together in anticipation, knowing I'm about to send him into a tizzy.

"You'll never guess who's here right now," I say, attempting to goad him into action. I point to Wannstedt and his wife sitting in a corner booth. Ditka pivots and stares at the couple for a few seconds. I'm sure he's thinking, "Well, this is awkward."

With a devilish look in my eyes, I say, "What a coincidence."

Ditka whispers to his wife, likely something about whether they should stay or leave.

I give them no say in the matter.

"Maybe you should join them?" I suggest, nudging him on with a subtle nod in the direction of Wannstedt's booth.

Being the snake charmer that I am, the Ditkas opt to stay. The old coach walks over to the new coach's table by himself, leaving his wife behind with me. I watch the two men shake hands and strike up a conversation. A minute later, Ditka waves his wife Diana over. They sit and join Wanny and his wife. There appears to be no battle brewing.

"Where's the damn friction?" I wonder.

The next thing I know, Ditka points me out to Wannstedt, identifying me as the culprit responsible for their chance meeting. My eyes go vertical from the sudden unwanted attention. Suddenly it dawns on me that these two brawny Bear coaches could beat the crap out of me.

I'm ready to duck out of the place, but Wanny responds to my presence with a friendly wave of the hand, as if to say...

Thank you, Mr. Leslie, for doing this.

I return his acknowledgment with a deferential bow of my head. Soon I'm seated on the other side of a crowded horseshoe bar, providing me with the cover needed to safely observe the Ditkas and Wannstedts. For the next two hours, I watch the two couples eat, drink and banter.

And that's how Da Coach and Wanny became good friends.

I was the guy who orchestrated the whole thing. It might have started out as a gag on my part. But it initiated a friendship that continued past 2005 when Ditka helped Wannstedt get his head-coaching job at Pitt, Ditka's alma mater.

As I look back on it now, I've had a knack for bringing conflicted people together my whole life.[1] I have no way of knowing if I can do the same for the Israelis and the Palestinians.

But I'm willing to try.

Just tell me where the restaurant is.

---

1. They weren't close friends themselves, but Steve and Claudia hung out together within a much larger circle of friends. Nobody other than me knew they had crushes on one another—an infatuation that had turned into love as the months passed. Fearful that one or the other didn't share the same romantic feelings, neither would dare make the first move. It was turning into a near-tragic love story when I finally intervened. I spoke to each privately and divulged the truth—how Steve felt about Claudia and how Claudia felt about Steve. The two were married for nearly fifty years before Steve had that damn fatal heart attack of his.

16

I was known as the polished tipper.
(How to reward waiters for putting up with obnoxious diners.)

A LITTLE SOMETHING ON etiquette, Rrricardo style.

When it comes to dining out, I'm always on my best behavior. That's true whether I eat with my fingers, talk while I'm chewing, or catch crumbs on my belly.

I abide by an unwritten code of conduct—dreamt up by myself—that states that one should act with restraint when dining out.

To my convoluted way of thinking (aren't all brains convoluted?), restaurateurs are just as worthy of having appreciative diners as customers are deserving of enjoying a decent meal.

For that reason, when I walk into a restaurant, I conduct myself in a refined fashion, best exemplified by the following list of Waspish-like manners.

I never ask for the second table first.

The one next to the urinals is fine.

I never complain if I'm seated beneath an air conditioning duct.

A slight winter breeze can be invigorating.

I never send food back to the kitchen.

And neither should you, if you know what's—ptui—good for you.

And I only question the bill if there's an unmistakable slip-up, like the time a local Chicago eatery charged me for my family's dinner, plus the four meals at the neighboring table.

Even then, I gave my obligatory twenty percent tip.

You'd think with all the restrictions I place upon myself when dining out, it wouldn't be too much to expect a wee something in return. Nothing special like singing waiters, though I do appreciate a well-sung aria like the one performed every Christmas at the Italian trattoria a few miles down the road from me.

No, all I ask is that I receive the kind of service reminiscent of a bygone era.

When waiters didn't introduce themselves.

Hello, my name is Felix. Can I be your bff this evening?

When waiters set down everyone's plate at the same time.

The chef says your meal will be ready tomorrow at three-fifteen.

And when waiters were attentive to your every need.

Can you pay me now? My shift's over.

Oh, what I'd give for a waiter like the ones we used to have in the good old days.

Fortunately, I didn't have to give up a thing when it finally happened in 2004.

The waiter may have just been a kid in his twenties, but there was something extraordinary about him. He had a special sensitivity to the needs of the diner—a savoir-faire if you will—that led me to believe he was more than a waiter. He was a fellow student of human understanding.

I couldn't help but appreciate his style, not knowing that the best was yet to come.

By dinner's end, I noticed he had serviced our table without introduction, interruption, or intercourse, "The Three I's of Wrongful Waitering," as laid out by that Ricardo guy I spoke of earlier.

As my own kids appreciate—*and my wife doesn't*—I often reward and punish people based on how they act. One example is drivers who honk the second the light turns green.

"They must be punished." I utter to my two sons in the best Peter Lorre imitation I can muster.[1]

I accelerate ever so slowly to annoy these honkers further.

Then there are those shoppers who wait until the last item is rung up on the register before rummaging through their purses for their wallets. Don't they know others are waiting in line?

"They-eey mu-ust be-ee pun-niished," I say to my wife, mimicking the quivering voice of Kathryn Hepburn.

I ask those shoppers if they'd rather have me pay for their purchase.

And don't even get me started on moviegoers who take their sweet time at the concession stand.

"Those dirty rats must be punished." I say to my daughter, who's never heard James Cagney speak before.

I subtly start humming, "The Longest Time" by Billy Joel to speed them up.[2]

But when my perfect young waiter came around with the check, I knew he had to be rewarded beyond the ordinary. If anyone deserved a big tip, he did. I scribbled one on the bill.

"You were the best waiter I've ever had. It should serve you well in the future."

Yes, my tip was a little positive reinforcement from a total stranger. I slipped it inside the billfold, along with my customary twenty percent tip.

My wife said I was cheap.

But when I returned to that restaurant weeks later, the same waiter ran up front to tell the host to seat us at his table. He soon came over and thanked me for the note I had penned. He said nobody had done that before.

That evening, I once again got excellent service. But this time I gave him a twenty-five percent tip with another short note.

"Well played," it read.

I cherish my anonymity, but I was pleased to see my dining experience written up in the Chicago Tribune the following week. The reporter called me "The Polished Tipper."

And two radio talk show hosts that morning discussed my tipping technique over the air. That's what peoples' imaginations will do when they come in contact with the *unexpected*.

It results in people taking notice of you. And getting noticed is often the first step in moving ahead in the world.

As for my waiter, I'd like to think he went far in life. He earned it.

That's more than I can say for myself.

I cheated.

---

1. Peter Lorre was a legendary character actor who spoke in a sleepy, ghoulish voice. I often imitated him as a kid. Also, James Cagney and Katharine Hepburn, (the latter not in drag, though).

2. I no longer go to the movies. They force you to choose your seat before you enter the theater. Only to discover you're sitting too close or too far back. Hate that. But who cares what I think?

17

I got a C- on an A+ term paper.
(How to get the most out of a worthless college education.)

SINCE THERE'S NO WAY to convince you that cheating is okay—or that cheaters can prosper—the least I ask is that you be reasonable about some of my more underhanded undertakings.

Though I didn't always play things fair and square in my personal and business affairs, I never cheated in a way that would qualify me as a lowlife.

I never cheated on my taxes.

I wouldn't even know how to do it.

I never cheated on my wife.

Love you, sweetie.

And I never cheated at cards.

I was more likely the victim of poker table shenanigans.

The only cheating I ever did was restricted to the classroom. So, at worst, I was merely cheating myself. That's what teachers used to say to cheaters back in the old days. They were right too, if I'm willingly going to acknowledge all the gaps in my education.

Looking back on my school years now, I regret many of my youthful indiscretions. But in fairness to me, it's possible the cheating I did wasn't my fault. I may have been pushed into it. You know, the whole nature-nurture thing.

I've been told that most shrinks would attribute my poor grades to some childhood psychological trauma. If so, I'm ignorant of what that damaging blow was—or who did it.

I'm also unaware of anything my parents might have done to throw my brain out of whack. They never whipped me, tied me up in the closet, or chained me to a basement wall.

That said, my mom did slap me in the face once. It was a split-second after I called her an old bag. She was thirty-six at the time. I was eleven. But I may have had that punch coming. Besides, by that time I was already cheating in school.

That's why I always sat next to the smartest kids in class.

Now that I think of it, there may be one other possible explanation for my classroom shortcomings. My mom once alluded to a misbehaving teenage babysitter who had given me crabs as a toddler. Evidently, the critters attached themselves to my eyelids. I never asked my mother what else that babysitter may have done to me besides sitting on my face. I really didn't want to know.

I peeked inside her va-ja-na, mama. Icky.

Extreme babysitting trauma may not work for you. But it's the best alibi I've got to explain my penchant for cheating in school. Though I suspect many of my teachers would argue that it was my *fatal flaw*, as described in chapter eleven, that had more to do with it.

Today, it's crazy to even attempt to cheat. Colleges use plagiarizing software to catch copycats and kick them out of school. But cheating was prevalent during my college days. Most schools didn't even have honor codes yet, so I had no qualms about doing whatever was necessary to increase any grade I could.

Including the passing grade I desperately needed in my Sociology 304 class.

I had brought this dilemma upon myself when my D average had fallen perilously close to an F. If I failed the course, I would have fallen four credits shy of meeting my major requirement.

As well as four hours short of graduating.

And that would have placed me in a precarious position.

To pass the course, I would either have had to pass the final exam—not a likely outcome since I had never purchased the textbook or attended most classes—or I had to ace my end-of-year research paper. Also doubtful since I had never written an A paper through seventeen years of schooling.

But then a serendipitous, life-saving opportunity arose.

It's time to remind readers that Darwin's "survival of the fittest" doesn't come with a morality clause.

At the last second, my friend Steve Walter, (the same Steve from the footnote in Chapter 15), came to the rescue and saved my stupid ass. Though he'd never cheat himself, Steve was no goody-two-shoes, meaning he wasn't above aiding and abetting a petty cheater by gifting him a previously-written term paper.

Steve was no slouch in the classroom either. He was co-valedictorian at the University of Illinois in 1969. Got straight A's in college. Minus one B that he received his final semester. That was the reason why Steve had a "co-" in front of his valedictorian certificate.

When he went on to become a judge years later, he sat on the bench with great distinction, securing the reputation of an impartial and fair-minded jurist.

Even Steven.

That's who Steve was.

In juxtaposition to uneven Rick.

That's who Rick is.

I headed over to Steve's apartment to borrow the thirty-seven-page term paper he had written a year earlier for his Poly Sci class. I saw a big red A+ on it. Perfect, I thought. Steve swore he had perused my class curriculum to make sure the paper was a good fit for my sociology class. I took it home, retyped it, and handed it in as my own.

Look, if you're going to cheat, you might as well cheat with help from the best.

I had high hopes for an A. But when I got the paper back, the front page was marked with an ugly C-minus across the top. That's got to be a mistake, I thought. I had gotten a slightly below average grade on the same research paper Steve had gotten an A+ on.

Though I had now raised my overall grade from a low D to a higher D, I knew that wouldn't be good enough to pass the course—and graduate— once I failed the final exam. And that's what would have taken place if life always went according to script.

But sometimes *unexpected* twists of fate intervene to save sorry asses. My twist preordained that I would never have to take the final exam because of the following chain of events.

Toward the end of that semester, campus unrest had grown across the country in protest of Nixon's invasion of Cambodia. Bedlam ensued. Everybody was rioting everywhere, hurling rocks through storefront windows, overturning parked cars, and setting fire to American flags. Within a week, the rioters at Illinois had seized the administration building. The National Guard was called in to bash heads.

Then miracle of miracles!

All the campus turmoil prompted the school president to shut down classes two weeks before the semester ended.

Lucky me.

That meant final exams would be cancelled and every course would be graded pass/fail. And without a final exam to help me fail the course, I wound up passing it.

As for Steve, I never told him I had gotten a C- on his A+ term paper. I didn't want him to know somebody had considered him slightly below average in any way. It might have hurt his feelings.

On the flip side, I was used to it.

When Steve died of a massive coronary a few years back, I was unable to come to his rescue and save *his* sorry ass. There were no miracles in his script. But that shouldn't come as a surprise to anyone. Some people never get the kudos they deserve.

Nor the disapprovals they merit.

Come hell or high water, ain't that the truth.

18

I made water towers a matter of life and death.
(How to turn the ordinary into the extraordinary.)

WAS I DYING OF boredom?

Or was I just driving through small-town America when I came across a water tower off in the distance? I had never given these towers a second thought for the same reason you haven't. Water towers are mundane. As boring as boring can be. Everything I knew about them could be summed up this way.

They're everywhere—and they hold water. And that's *that.* I don't remember why I gave these towers a second thought that day. But I did.

Hold water for what, I pondered? Drinking water?

On *third* thought, I realized that didn't make sense. Why would we need towers filled with water when there are lakes, rivers, wells or reservoirs nearby? Even if the tower's water supply was for emergency use—on the offhand chance somebody poisoned the local water supply—why build them high above the ground?

C'mon, how many teenagers are going to climb up a tower and steal a town's water?

On *fourth* thought, wouldn't we all be better off if the towers weren't towers at all? Just oversized jugs stationed at street level. That way water would be more accessible to those dying of thirst. Like for guys buying Big Gulps at Seven-Elevens. Or for camels with two humps.

Meh, even water tower humor is dull.

With few regrets, I couldn't think of a single reason why water towers might be interesting to anyone. Until a *fifth* thought struck me.

Towns often decorate their towers to represent something their community is known for, like the rose-painted one in Rosemont, Illinois. Or the pumpkin-shaped one in Circleville, Ohio.

Otherwise, most towers have the town's name stenciled on it, so out-of-towners will always know where they are—sort of a backup ID system for visitors missing the community's signage when they drive into town.

With no other purpose in mind, I had reached a literary dead end. Until I did a hasty mental calculation—a *sixth* thought—and came across a new direction to take. It necessitated a little water tower philosophizing to get there.

If water towers exist, then there must be water tower companies that build them. And if there are water tower companies, then there must be water tower salesmen.

On *seventh* thought, I imagined the following sales pitch.

"This model here is the twenty-one-ton XR-150. It comes as a basketball, a peach, a globe, a baseball, or the likeness of Rick's damaged right testicle from falling into a sump pump in a McDonald's basement when he was twenty-three."

I snickered at my *seventh* thought, as you might be doing now. The notion that this might be a lighthearted *Today* show segment excited me.

I felt a rush go through my body.

Was I having a stroke?

No. It was just my blood pressure rising when I found a water tower shaped like a coffee pot in Stanton, Iowa—the hometown of Mrs. Folger of TV commercial acclaim. Without missing a beat, my partner blurted out, "Pour a cup from up there and good luck holding onto the cup."

I immediately grasped the connection—my *eighth* thought about water towers. They store water above ground to create water pressure below ground. The revelation caused my heart to skip a beat.

Could it be a heart attack?

Uh-uh. It was just my *ninth* thought. That I better call a water tower company for answers.

When I did, they said, "A water tower's main purpose is to increase water pressure to hydrants when there's a fire in town."

There you have it. The reason for all those *blah* water towers across the landscape of America. They're a matter of utmost gravity, meaning that the purpose they serve isn't just of great concern to us all, but that gravity is the force that makes water towers work. Without them, firemen wouldn't be guaranteed the water pressure needed to fight fires and save lives. My brain was ready to implode.

Did an aneurysm just pop in my head?

Or did I just uncover the elemental truth about water towers by delving deeper and deeper into their mysteries? Something most people don't have time for. Nor the inclination. But, thanks to all of my varied training, I can't stop my mind from going places where most others don't dare to go.

At least, not without the risk of appearing stupid.

I may not recognize the significance of all the building blocks of modern life. But we should all be more appreciative of people who figure out ways to better life.

It'd be wrong not to.

Which is why I quietly thank them every time I pass a water tower or a cell tower or a garbage truck or a sewer line. Because it takes no *tenth* thought to realize where our lives would be without the mundane things in it.

Including plain old vanilla.

19

I did the first national news story on vanilla.
(How to develop a nose for news that's really news.)

WHY DOES CHOCOLATE GET all the press?

How come the headlines always scream chocolate *this* and chocolate *that*? Why don't we hear of strawberry-aholics? Peach-aholics? Or rum raisin-aholics? I contemplated those questions and more when I got my umpteenth pitch for a chocolate story from a New York PR firm.

Ugh! Not again, I thought.

Then I opened the large box that came with it. I knew from experience that there would be some kind of bribe inside that carton to help convince me of their client's newsworthiness. (There always is when you're pitched a story with an accompanying package.)

I didn't have a clue what my payoff would be this time. But my eyes widened when I discovered a full-sized chocolate female leg inside.

In a laced silk stocking, no less.

Have I told you how much I love chocolate yet?

I love it more than women in silk stockings. Almost. But chocolate stories have been done to death. No way was I going to do another news feature about it. That would have been *old* news. Just the opposite of what real news is. Which is *new* news.

May I suggest that we call all old news *olds* from this day forward? And all new news *news?* That would help us differentiate between what's been told before from what hasn't, so we can concentrate all our efforts into differentiating *fake* news from *real* news.

As a former newsman, one of the skills I'm blessed with is getting to the core of things. Even if those things are uncommon, and often inconsequential.

In this particular situation, it was the truth about chocolate. The inconvenient truth as I soon discovered.

Inconvenient truths apply to more than climate change, you know.

It turns out chocolate is a fraud. It's not what it's made out to be. Vanilla is a far more popular flavor.

How's that for a little sugar rush?

And the misleading reportage doesn't stop there. Case in point: You can't even make good chocolate without adding vanilla. That's right. Every time you eat chocolate, you're also swallowing a tiny drop of vanilla. Bet you didn't know that chocolate relies on vanilla extract to enhance its taste.

Sort of like death depends on life ending before it can occur.

The understatement of the month award goes to—envelope, please...

But for chocolate dependency-sake alone, vanilla merits far more attention than it gets. And that's why I decided to do the first national news report on vanilla. I knew I had a winning idea on my hands before the story even aired, since a news feature on vanilla wouldn't be *olds*. It would be *news*.[1] Folks tune out *olds* (been there, seen that), causing a quandary for the news industry because pretty much everything going on is *olds*.

Oh, what is an honor-bound news producer to do?

You do what any crafty newsman or woman does. Convert *olds* into *news* by coming up with a fresh new angle, such as...

Female Chocolate Legs Can Lead to Diabetes.

Don't fall for it. The above headline is repeating the same old thing. Too much chocolate isn't good for you. But everyone already knows that. So how can that be *news?*

It can't. It's *olds.*

But news programs need to report lots of *olds* each day because there's never enough *news* to fill a complete hour. Not even a half-hour. Fifteen minutes a day seems about right. That's because *news* rarely happens unless something new actually occurs.

Something you've never heard or seen before.

Something so *unexpected* that it captures the attention and stirs the imagination from the get-go.

Like Category Five hurricanes.

Twos, threes and fours are so ordinary, don't you think?

Or tsunamis hitting nuclear power plants.

Tidal waves are so passé.

Or Near-Death Experiences.

The discovery of an afterlife would put CNN in ratings' heaven.

Or airplanes crashing into high-rise buildings. Or AI running amok. Or the housing market collapsing. Or a buffoon winning the presidency. Or the stock market crashing. Or runaway inflation. Or America coming to an end.

Please wake me up from my nap if any of the above happens.

"Shit! Most of them have." I promptly said to myself after writing the above sentences.

Those stories were so damned interesting. Titillating even. Much like anti-war movies having the unintended effect of making war look super-cool.

Maybe even twice as cool as plain old vanilla.

But, so far as stories go, the vanilla one takes no backseat to all of the aforementioned disasters. The nature of its flavor may not be Earth-shattering news, like a 10.2 earthquake, but it does have something in common with all the above examples.

It's *unexpected.*[2]

But that's only half the vanilla story.

Though I've never been a lover of metaphors, it's not lost on me that most everybody belongs to one of two groups. You're either a vanilla person who quietly goes about their work. Or a chocolate person who takes all the credit for it. (Please do *not* interpret the above analogy to be a racially motivated statement about uppity chocolate people.)

The previous sentence is directed at white supremacists who may—or may not—be reading this book.

It's sad that a vanilla guy like me never got paid as handsomely as his chocolate counterpart. But that was what I signed up for when I worked for the networks. (I also worked for ABC News for three years.) To dream up ideas nobody else had had before, like…

Many Adults Suffer from Childhood Learning Disabilities.

I came up with the above headline in 1992 when I was thinking about learning disabilities kids have. I knew if adults had them too, it would be news. But only if my hypothesis was correct. I called the psych department at Northwestern University. They concurred, saying many grownups continue to endure the same learning disabilities they had as kids. Not good news for them, because the older you get, the worse the impediment can get.

Potentially even leading to suicide.

"Now that is news," said the ABC 20/20 segment producer when I pitched it to her.[3] But it never got produced. Nobody takes the second guy in command—the *vanilla* guy—seriously.

Who cares if I was Mr. Spock to Star Trek's Captain Kirk.[4] It could have been worse. Much worse. I could have been the strawberry in Neapolitan ice cream—the flavor that's always getting its ass kicked.

Instead of licked.

But comic relief aside, I'm kind of angry that I never became a chocolate person. After all, I love chocolate. It's not right that there's no correlation between flavor preferences and favored treatment preferences.

Getting right to the core of it, life isn't fair.

I've pretty much gotten over it. But not everyone is so lucky.

---

1. When's the last time you saw a story on vanilla?

2. Doing the *unexpected* entertains others. But please don't do anything stupid, like hold up a bank and hand over your *own* money rather than stealing theirs. If you're that dense, however, don't be surprised if the bank's CCTV footage goes viral and you become famous. Here's a heads up. Should that happen, book publishers will likely want to know your story. You'll wind up with a book deal and make five or six million bucks from sales. Goddammit! Life isn't fair at all. Look, it was my idea to rob the bank without stealing a dime in the first place. And it's just not right that somebody else is getting rich off of my idea. Woe is me.

3. My story about adult learning disabilities is no longer *news*. It's been covered quite a few times since I first pitched it to 20/20 in 1992.

4. Soon after I started working for NBC, I developed a *Jingles' Complex*. For those too young to remember, Jingles was the fictional sidekick in the *Adventures of Wild Bill Hickok*, the TV version of Hickok's life that aired in the 1950s. As the fat and bumbling cowpoke who always got himself into trouble, Jingles provided the comic relief for the program. If Bill had been murdered on the show—as he had been in real life—Jingles probably would've been passed over for promotion and reassigned to a new Marshall. Lacking gravitas, nobody took Jingles seriously. That describes Jingles as he rode off into the sunset after each episode. And that defines me. "*Hey, Wild Bill, wait for Meeeeee!*

20

I went to a prostitute and came home a virgin.
(How to correct mistakes before you make them.)

TEENAGE HORMONES BEING what they are, the male sex drive can activate at the most inopportune of times.

One such time was the mid-sixties, when high school girls wore flared skirts and tight sweaters, fragrant perfumes and flirty smiles.

In those days, I didn't have to watch any raunchy teenage sex comedy to know sex was in the air. It was everywhere. Often causing me to stand erect in the hallways.

Without once being complimented for good posture, I might add.

And that was the extent of my teenage sex life.

Though that's not entirely true, since I did fantasize about these girls a lot. Mainly at night. Under the covers. But sometimes in the shower.

And maybe twice in the utility room down in the basement.

Hey, the furnace was hot.

Even if I wasn't.

I was in fact chubby at that time. And in my opinion, my heft made me more an object of ridicule than of desire. That's what a poor self-image in high school can do to a teenager.

But when it came to girls, I had an even bigger problem than the extra forty pounds I carried. I was also way too fussy about the girls I wanted to go out with, only falling for the prettiest of them.

As a result. I never went out on a real date in high school.

Knowing what I know now, I was stupid for not asking out any of the lesser beauties. Many grew into their looks, often turning into hot stuff as they matured.

But during high school, I was focused on the few luscious beauties that passed me in the halls each day. Without making any eye contact with me.

It's weird how the truth can change over time. Yet pretty high school girls remain the same.

They were way out of my league. I write *were* because at my fiftieth high school reunion these same women told me they would have gone out with me in high school if I had asked.

Dumb me then.[1]

Dumb me now.

Because even today, I remain clueless about female wants, needs and desires.

But I'm getting way ahead of myself.

Or is it way behind, since I'm writing about the years after high school as well as the years before now? Like when I was a freshman in college. Back then, even with a sizable weight loss, I couldn't get a woman to do anything more than make out.

They'd moan, "No, no, stop, please stop," as my hands neared their prized possessions.

Like the righteous guy I was, I always stopped.[2]

It was apparent I had to take matters into my own figurative hands if I wanted to get things done. I called a prostitute and scheduled an appointment on the eve of my nineteenth birthday.

This is where my story does a one-eighty.

Real life does that sometimes.

I assumed I was going to a house of ill repute. Instead, I pulled up to a house in ill repair, situated in the most dangerous and impoverished neighborhood of Champaign-Urbana. I was scared half to death, but who wouldn't be in a gang-infested section of town?

If I had been murdered, the police would have laughed about another college-aged male virgin dying for sex.

But I was so desperate for intercourse that I walked down a dark alley, crossing paths with a couple of *black cats*, until I reached the back of the house. That's how powerful a sex drive can be in a young man. It's stronger than the threat of physical violence; more powerful than the fear of mental anguish.

However, it's not as incapacitating as a slobbering dog licking your naked body while trying to make love to a woman on her living room floor.

But that wouldn't take place for a couple of years yet.

As for this moment in time, I knocked on the backdoor, half ajar, and a man's voice yelled out for me to come in. I stepped into a barren, well-worn room with holes in the plaster walls, empty beer cans strewn about, and the unmistakable odor of cat feces wafting throughout.

On a tattered brown sofa sat an older man and woman. They looked to be in their forties. I assumed they were the parents of the prostitute, but when I saw the baby girl nestled between them, I realized they were grandparents too.

Let's have a happy sing-along, boys and girls. It's family time in the Williams' household.

Grandpa spoke up first. "She'll be with you in a few. Grab a chair if you want."

I sat and waited, using this free time to assess the family's situation. It didn't seem promising at all. I figured the grandparents' job was to babysit while I did the dirty deed with their daughter. I wondered if this was going to be the baby's fate too.

That thought made me uncomfortable. Even worse, grandma and grandpa were watching *Mission: Impossible* on TV. I took that as a bad omen—a portent of nothing to *come* in my future.

Or, far more likely, nothing to come in theirs.

Because with no husband or father in the picture, someone had to pay the rent, buy the groceries, and feed the baby. That someone was apparently my prostitute.

And then came the bombshell.

A girl walked out of the bedroom. A young girl. Sixteen at most. Wearing no flared skirt. No tight sweater. No fragrant perfume. No flirty smile.

Only a flimsy nightgown that couldn't begin to cover the truth of her existence.

That was the moment I discovered the male sex drive wasn't stronger than first time exposure to abject poverty. Sex had lost its appeal. I wanted no part of this. There was no pleasure to be taken from a desperate teenage girl in dire straits.

And she didn't even have to say "no" to get me to stop.

I had to get out of there fast. Offering no excuse, I handed the young prostitute the ten dollars I owed and said, "I can't do this."

She gave me an odd look, like I was speaking of impotence. But that was okay. I turned to her parents and apologized. "Sorry to be a bother. But thanks anyway."

I hurried out the door where the cool, late autumn air made me carefree and drunk again. As I drove home that night, I discovered I was happier living in a fantasy world of high school sweethearts that never were than in the grimmest of realities that often are.

Even if only for a brief moment.

---

1. Unfortunately for me, I learned how to speak to high school girls 50 years too late.

2. I had one successful outing as a bad boy. Within minutes of meeting this scorching hot blond at a neighbor's party, I asked her to go upstairs to my place. She emphatically said, "No, I'm not that kind of girl." It was a conversation stopper. But not the end of such boldness. For soon after, she tapped me on the shoulder and said she had changed her mind. Apparently, this girl had a bit of *bad* girl in her. In the morning, we showered and I washed her hair—being the good guy that I truly was. She liked that a lot, proving she was indeed a "good girl" at heart. Afterward, we got dressed and I took my future wife—the mother of my three children—to breakfast. If there's a lesson to be gleaned from this "how we met" story, it's this: sometimes you've got to break free of your comfort zone. Sometimes you've got to be a little naughty to be nice.

21

I was a Boy Scout for a day.
(How to get the better of control freaks)

I KNEW THE BOY SCOUTS wouldn't be a good fit for me when I showed up at the initial meeting.

I was the only one there.

I had assumed all my Cub Scout friends would come, but they evidently knew something I didn't. The Boy Scouts were kind of lame. And that's why I sat by myself in a large living room across the table from some pimply-faced scout leader who immediately began to annoy me with his many nervous habits.

He tapped his fingertips on the table in rapid syncopation.

Stop it! (I thought but didn't say.)

He cracked his knuckles to no end.

Please stop it. (I thought but didn't say.)

And he cleared his throat every few seconds.

Damn! Will you stop it already? (I thought but didn't say.)

All those little irritants were carrying on while he tried to sell me on the benefits of scouting.

"It builds moral fiber," he said. "You prepared for that?"

I wasn't prepared for that.

I should have excused myself then and there, being the immoral twelve-year-old that I was. But I didn't know how to extricate myself from unwelcome situations at that time without coming across as rude.

It's an affliction I've never quite outgrown.

I nodded *yes* to his above question, but only because it couldn't be answered any other way. I was trapped by his words.

Trapped into agreeing.

Trapped into going along with everything he had to say.

When he finished his entire presentation and said, "Be prepared. That's our motto. A great way to live life, don't you think?"

I once again nodded *yes*.

Even though I wanted to say, "Thanks for everything. I'm going home now. See you never again."

It would have been so much easier if I had. Then the scout leader wouldn't have slid the application across the table. And I wouldn't have been artfully manipulated by a weird fifteen-year-old kid into becoming a Boy Scout.

Even though I didn't want to be a Boy Scout.

Besides, I knew I could never muster up the energy to follow through on any activity requiring preparation.

It's the reason why I quit guitar lessons in sixth grade.

How was I to know I'd become a singer/songwriter eleven years later?

The reason why I ditched Hebrew School in favor of the immediate gratification of after school sports in seventh grade.

It turned out to be a poor financial decision with no Bar Mitzvah money forthcoming.

And the reason why I couldn't build model planes and tanks without making a gluey mess.

Mom, I'm feeling kind of strange right now.

107

At twelve, I hadn't yet gained any awareness of my personal flaws—or the regrets that would later develop. The following day, a Saturday—my first as a Scout—the two of us hiked to the nearby forest preserves. The scout leader had told me to come equipped with matches, a flashlight, and a pocketknife for whittling or playing Mumblety Peg.[1]

But he had mentioned nothing of boots, gloves, scarves and hats.[2] Unnecessary items in the dead of winter when the sun is shining bright, which makes the air feel warmer than it really is.[3] But as we marched into the woods, the sun got blocked from view and a stiff chill set in.

That wouldn't have been a problem, however, if hadn't been for the sudden change in the weather. The temperature plummeted and it began to blizzard.

I wasn't prepared for that.

The scout leader said nothing about the way I had dressed. But I knew that he knew that I had come unprepared my first day as a Boy Scout.

Even a campfire didn't help. My ears went numb, my body shivered, and my teeth chattered in rhythm to a Ginger Baker[4] drum solo. I was ready to leave after twenty minutes, but I wasn't brave enough to get up and go. I needed to wait for just the right moment to *unfollow* the leader.

That opportunity took forever.

I sat on a log like the bump I was. And sat…and sat… and sat.

Until I began to sweat and cough and ache. After forty minutes of scouting, I needed to go home. But I found it impossible to sever myself from the controls of the scout leader. Every sentence he spoke ended with a question, obliging me to respond in the affirmative—the way he wanted me to answer.

Like…

"I love scouting. It's so much fun, isn't it?"

And...

"I brought along some hot dogs and marshmallows. You don't mind digging up a couple of sticks for us, do you?"

As well as...

"I'm so glad you joined. Some kids don't get scouting. But I can tell you like this, right?"

It was all so easy for him to say. He was outfitted to survive weeks in a frozen tundra. Whereas I was ill by then. Snot was pouring from my nose, freezing on my face before I could wipe it off on my jacket sleeve. The scout leader, being the leader of young men that he was, readily diagnosed my condition.

"You look cold. You gonna be okay?"

I shook my head no.

"Better do some Jumping Jacks. That'll warm you up."

I had never heard the F-bomb used to voice strong displeasure before. But if I had, I would have screamed it out right then.

Instead, I leaned over and puked.

The scout leader wasn't prepared for that.

I pushed myself up from the log and told him I was going home. And just like that, I was free.

Free of his stupid comments.

Free of his idiosyncrasies.

And free to call my own shots and do what I wanted to do all along.

Crawl under the covers at home.

I walked out of the snowy woods that Saturday afternoon, having faced my first ever control freak. I wish I could say I was never dominated by anybody else again. But it would take years for me to take control and weed these individuals from my life.

As for twelve-year-old me, I quit the Boy Scouts on Sunday.

Missed school with the stomach flu on Monday, Tuesday and Wednesday.

And on Saturday—thirty-seven years later—I once again broke the Scout's motto.

But a guy's got to do what a guy's got to do, right?

---

1. Mumblety-peg was a game requiring young boys to fling their pocketknives as close to one of their feet as possible. Once well-meaning mothers discovered what their little fellas were up to, they were hell-bent on banning the game from this Earth. In later years, these same moms forced young bicycle riders to wear helmets too. God knows how many toes and front teeth have been saved thanks to moms.

2. I often go out in the winter without a coat or hat. It's one of the benefits of being a ruggedly handsome indoorsman.

3. The Wind Chill Index hadn't yet been introduced in 1958. In those days, people believed the temperature outside was the *actual* temperature outside, irrespective of any breeze in the air. But if the WCI is indeed an accurate measurement of what the outside air feels like on your skin, why doesn't it feel like it's freezing outside when the temperature is seventy, and the wind is blowing a 100 mph?

4. Ginger Baker was a superstar drummer in the 60s and 70's who played alongside Eric Clapton in the band *Cream*.

22

I went in the woods unprepared.
(How to clean up all of life's messes.)

IT'S SATURDAY MORNING. A day made as much for Jack Frost as Robert Frost.

Heavy snow has blanketed our storybook town. The ground glistens like silvery glass from a sky free of clouds. It's a perfect day for traipsing through crisp, snowy woods with my seven-year-old son Jamie, before going back home to a mug of mom's hot cocoa.

Jamie has never gone hiking in the woods. He imagines it to be a great adventure. I plan to take him to the same forest preserves I went to as a Boy Scout.

It's far closer to the house I live in than the house I grew up in.

Dressed in parkas, scarves, gloves, boots and hats, Jamie and I are well prepared for our short outing. Our ragamuffin dog Rags, in his trademark red- and white-checkered bandana, tags along.

We drive over and hike about a tenth of a mile into the woods—halfway between the road and an adjacent golf course. But we might as well be a million miles from home. That's what solitude in the woods can do for you.

Thank you, Mr. Thoreau.

We come upon a tree stump and sit. I put my arm around my son as much to cuddle him as to warm him up. That's when the fiber—not the strong moral type but the kind that came from that morning's two bowls of Raisin Bran—starts to take effect.

I pass some gas.

Jamie laughs. Kids find farts funny. (And so do I.)

But then—*ugh*—I develop a stomachache. And with it comes a sudden urge to go. My intestinal fortitude is about to be tested. The first cramp strikes without warning, causing me to reflexively shut my butt hole tight. Yeah, it hurts. But I imagine it to be no worse than a female contraction.

One day I'm sure I'll regret making that birthing comparison.

But who can think straight when their thoughts are fueled by agony? For with each succeeding cramp, my sphincter muscle spasms out of control. Until I can't hold it in any longer. I have to answer nature's call—like now!

Nurse, my rectum is fully dilated!

I quickly consider the alternatives. Jamie and I can either call it a day and head home to the comfort of my own toilet. Or I can do the nasty in the woods. The decision is made for me when I can't control my urge to go any longer.

Doubled up in excruciating pain, I pull down my jeans and squat.

Jamie is doubled up in laughter. He has never seen a grown-up do this. But he will not be scarred for life, even though my wife and daughter—who will both hear the story shortly—think otherwise.

But why would Jamie be hurt by something as natural as a man going in the woods? Unless that something keeps going and going and going. Until one end is scraping the ground and the other is still escaping the butt.

You've now reached the rear end of this book. But wait, there's more.

Standing tall, a foot and a half above the snow line, my stool looks like a Saturn II rocket on a launching pad about to take off.

But Houston, we have a problem.

It turns out the dude is a dud.

The missile sizzles as it slowly sinks into—and, in due course, under—the snow.

Jamie is hysterical now. And so am I, in a non-laughing sort of way. It appears the missile hasn't exited the silo as smoothly as I had hoped. I have no Kleenex with me to wipe myself. I scour that neck of the woods—and see nothing to use. Neither leaf nor litter is to be seen.

Where's a reliable, non-biodegradable, fast-food hamburger wrapper when you need one?

Once again—loosely interpreted—I've gone in the woods unprepared. Just like I did thirty-seven years earlier when I was a Boy Scout for a day.

Jamie falls to his knees in delight. Rags barks in agreement. I'm still squatting, fearful of getting any *caca*—I had eaten Mexican food the night before—on my pants. I go into a momentary trance to think.[1]

What do I do? What do I do?

I could use my shirt, I surmise. But I dread driving home bare-chested in winter. I mean, it's not like I'm built like Fabio.[2] But it appears I have no other option but to grin and bare it.

That's what I'm about to do when I ask Jamie if he has any other ideas. I believe the question is an excellent critical thinking exercise for him. He advises me to use my knitted scarf. I tell Jamie, "Good idea." But no way is the scarf up to the task.

The shirt is my only option. I take off my parka and toss it on the snow. Rags wanders over and lies down on it for warmth. And that's when I see the checkered bandana around his neck. His scarf is exactly what my tush needs. I ask Jamie to untie it and bring it over. My only concern is that I'm allergic to dogs, even though I own one.

Don't ask me why? Ask my wife why?

I'm not sure what effect the bandana might have on my digestive tract. A few days of a deep, inaccessible itch perhaps?

"Oh, what the hell," I say to Jamie. And I begin to wipe up the mess. It works fine.

Upon applying the finishing touch, I bury the kerchief in the snow. I pity the next father and son who might mosey along these very parts in need of a good asswipe. But a few good thunderstorms should give the bandana a good washing. And leave it as good as new after the spring thaw.

In any event, that is what I tell myself. I almost believe it too.

Meanwhile, Jamie's fifteen-minute adventure has left him tuckered out. He says his belly is hurting from laughing so hard. We call it a day.

Walking back to the car, I'm reminded of the first time I found myself on the short end of readiness in these woods. Long forgotten words pop into my head out of nowhere. Next thing I know I'm reciting the Boy Scout oath.

"On my honor, I will do my best to do my *duty*…"

Jamie doesn't yet understand the humor in these words. But they're not lost on me. And neither should they be lost on you. I did my duty that day. I went in the woods. Unprepared. And walked out a *Man Scout*.

"What's a Man Scout, you ask? It's a guy unprepared for everything. But realizes with enough thought—and good fortune—there's a solution to most everything.

Mine just happened to be a memorable one. Almost as unforgettable as the evening I spent with Bill Murray.

If I remember correctly.

---

1. I tend to tune out the world around me when I think. I think that's why most people who don't know me don't know what to think when they meet me. Whaa?

2. Fabio, an Italian fashion model, appeared on the covers of dozens of romance novels throughout the 1980s and 1990s.

23

I spent an unforgettable night with Bill Murray.
(How to be just as memorable as any celebrity.)

I'M PRETTY SURE I hung out with actor Bill Murray one night.

Scratch that.

I unequivocally hung out with Bill Murray one evening. I just can't remember much about it.

You'd think an evening spent with Bill would be indelibly etched in my mind. But it's not. I can't remember one thing about our time together.

Nothing Bill said stands out.

Nothing he did sticks out.

Looking back on that night is like staring at an out-of-focus snapshot rather than the vivid color movie it should be. But our little adventure together wasn't even filmed in black and white. Just black. As in blackout. Total blackout.

That's right. I have no memory of watching Bill Murray perform at *Second City* earlier that evening. But I do recall going there with my best friend Lee. Of that much, I'm certain.

Not long ago I spoke to Lee about our night with Bill to see if he remembered anything more about it. He didn't. He only remembered the same thing I did.

Before I get to that "same thing," I've got to come clean about something. I don't wish to belittle *Second City*, but I seldom went to shows there because I never liked their improvisational humor. The skits always ended like Beethoven's Tenth Symphony.

Unfinished. With no *unexpected* punchlines to make audiences laugh hard.

To this day I don't find unfunny comedy funny.

Unless I'm the one writing it, which will appear later in this novel memoir.

As for now, you might wonder why I chose to go to *Second City* that night, though I hated it. It must have been because I knew a guy named Guy, who was the house piano player providing the comedy troupe's background music in the seventies. He likely gave me comp tickets to the show.

Otherwise, I never would have gone.

But I did go.

And that must have been the same night I caroused around town with Murray until ten the following morning.

It's all beginning to make sense now. But what was Betty Thomas doing with us?

This is not the start of a literary dream sequence. It's just me being myself.

Betty shouldn't need any introduction. She became famous for playing Officer Lucy Bates in *Hill Street Blues* before continuing on as an award-winning film director. But I can't remember why she joined us that evening?

Or how we even met.

Surprisingly, I can't remember meeting Bill either.

It could have occurred backstage after the performance.

Or on the street in front of the theater.

Either way, it doesn't matter. Somehow, we got together, and I'll leave it at that.

I wish my memories of that evening were as clear to me as the woman who derisively told me she had no desire to go out with me.[1] Ever. But they're not. They're draped under a rolling fog forever.

If you asked me what Bill and I did, I'd shrug my shoulders.

If you questioned where we went, I'd draw a blank.

If you pestered me about what we talked about, I'd wince and stammer.

Bill, Betty, Guy and Lee and I could have gotten stoned, ridden a grain elevator up and down, robbed a bank, or slapped mosquitoes on a muggy summer's night.

Or maybe Bill Murray put his arm around me and called me his best friend. If he did, I have yet to receive a single Christmas card from him.

Nor have I gotten a single invite to any Hollywood parties from Betty.

There are no two ways about it. I can't remember anything else about this most memorable evening with Bill, Betty and Deborah.

Deborah? Yeah, future TV star Deborah Harmon was also with us.

I'm fairly positive I don't suffer from dementia (yet), having passed all the mandatory Medicare memory tests—*apple, table, penny*—*house, lamb, grease*—*door, window, pizza*—at my doctor's office.[2]

I also know what I ate for dinner last night, where I parked my car this morning, and who my children are. Yet I can't remember more about that evening. Now entitled, "I spent a forgettable night with Bill Murray, Betty Thomas, and Deborah Harmon."

Why even bother to tell this story at all?

It's because something unforgettable did take place. Something so fresh, so unusual, so *unexpected* that it made Bill Murray's, Betty Thomas's and Deborah Harmon's presence irrelevant.

I walked *under* the Chicago River.

Not over, mind you. But under. I can't remember who uncovered the hidden entrance to the old coal tunnel. But all six of us walked in. The deeper we got, the darker it got.

Till it was pitch black.

Anyone who's watched horror movies knows nothing good happens in the dark—in the middle of the night—in a tunnel—to the chunkiest person in the party.

Me. Of course.

But I wasn't the one leading the way. I have no idea who was. I guess we all walked into the tunnel together, advancing with vigilance, cautious of any obstacles that might block our path.

We were halfway under the river, about to continue to the other side, when we stopped dead in our tracks. We heard something.

SHIT!

Something moving.

DOUBLE SHIT!!

Something alive.

TRIPLE SHIT!!!

Some sizable creature was in there with us.

DIARRHEA!!!!

We hustled out as fast as we could, crashing into one another like bumper cars, bouncing off walls like silly putty, and tripping over our feet as if ropes were tied around our ankles at a country picnic race. At that moment, nothing else mattered but our own survival.

Now that's something you don't forget.

We all made it out in one piece to whatever safety exists on Chicago's streets at four in the morning. And that's all I remember to this day.

The Bill Murrays, Betty Thomases and Deborah Harmons of this world can step in and out of your life, leaving no traces behind in their wake. But unknown creatures going boo in the night are engraved in your mind forever.

Sleep tight, Bill.

---

1. I met this girl Janet in a bar my junior year in college. We started talking and I thought we were getting along great, so I told her we should go out sometime. She looked at me and asked if I was Jewish. When I said yes, she replied, "I don't date Jewish guys." I figured she was an anti-semite, but then I discovered her last name was Goldberg. Why does this kind of crap always happen to me?

2. When you're over 65, doctors get paid extra to test the memory of their Medicare patients. They give old timers like me three words to memorize at the beginning of their exam, and then midway through, they ask you to repeat those three words. If you flunk the test, you have no hope of living into your nineties.

24

I'm afraid of my own dreams.
(How to live with the evil residing inside of you.)

I DON'T DREAM AS often as I used to.

Thank Goodness.

It may have something to do with the aging process. But whatever the cause, I now dream far less than I once did.

I only point this out in response to all the bad dreams I've had from childhood on. I don't mean *bad* in a nightmarish sort of way. (I've never dreamt of scary monsters.) But *bad* in the sense that all dreams have an inherently sinister nature. Even the good ones, such as flying high above treetops, can place you on treacherous grounds.

You might do a sudden nosedive if you wake up.

Even if I had been a patient of Sigmund Freud, it's a safe bet I still would have reached the same conclusion in dreams that I have in life. That my dreams haven't been entirely kind to me the past 26,300 or so nights. It's hard to explain the irreparable damages they've caused.

But due to a congenital writing disability,[1] I can describe in one short sentence, free of all psychobabble, what makes dreams so dangerous.

It's the power of suggestion.

Yes, the danger I face asleep is the same danger I find myself in when I read about the symptoms of a disease. Only to experience their onset before I finish reading. And that's why I fear dreams so much. These fantastical nightlife adventures enter my mind uninvited, offering me no say in the matter, no input in the storyline. In the final analysis, my opinions don't count when I'm dreaming. Just like they don't count in real life. What kind of bullshit is that?

It's nothing compared to their relentlessness.

They're like earworms crawling through my brain convolutions. It's near impossible to get them out of my head. Take this reoccurring nightmare that I had for a good ten years before the aging process… or my sleeping pill… reduced the number of dreams I now have.

> *It's nighttime. I'm walking along a street in Springfield, Illinois, when*
> *a street gang approaches. They ask me for money. I have none. Bang, bang.*
> *I'm lying in a pool of blood. My blood. Knowing I'm about to die.*

Just an ordinary nightmare, you say?

"Sorry," I say. "No way."

The first time I had that dream was the night before I had to go to Springfield for business. It ruined my trip. For two days, I was too afraid to venture outside. I've never gone back to Springfield since.

Screw that.

As a communications expert, I'm well aware of how simple it is to get the masses to think, say or do things *(buy another copy of my book)* that they would never say, think or do otherwise. *(buy another copy of my book)* I've been an easy target *(buy another copy of my book)* to this subliminal propaganda many times.

But I'm okay with advertisers trying to influence what I think and do. After all, they're just trying to convince me to buy stuff I don't want or need. If I work hard, I can tune out their message.

Dreams are different, however. They're not some external agent acting upon my free will. They're inside of me playing games with my head. And that scares the hell out of me.

How do you tune *yourself* out? You can't.

In dreamland, no viable options exist to stop these insidious nighttime invasions of the brain. It's mind control at its worst, as this next little anecdote demonstrates.

I once stopped having lunch with a co-worker because I dreamt he was mean to me the night before. I can't afford to lose any more friends because of my dreams.

I've already lost too many from being awake.

Going so far back as childhood, my dreams have never had my best interests at heart. They may have impressed me with abilities I never thought possible during the night. But come morning, seconds after discovering none of it was real, they've always depressed me.

That is why I can unambiguously state that dreams are nothing but a pack of lies.

What good does it do me to scoot along sidewalks with my feet off the ground? Only to discover that I can't really hover in the air?

How long must I continue to compose great symphonies in my sleep? That I can never recall awake?

What function does it serve for me to be hung like a horse in dreamland? If I'm an Amazonian shrunken head by morning.

But thanks to the aging process… or my sleeping pills… or the memory loss I'm experiencing… my dreams are now kept to a minimum.

And I'm better off for it.

Bedtime fantasies have brought me more frustration, more misery, more anguish than they've been worth. I readily admit that I have an occasional good dream now and then. But there's no way to enjoy it when you consider what dreams truly are.

Sorry to break the news, but after you strip away all the amazing stuff that happens during REM sleep, after you put aside all the lies they tell, you're left with nothing more than another *you* inside of *you* telling *you* what to do.

(Eerie music up)

What if *you* secretly hates you and convinces you to stand on real railroad tracks?

What if *you* teases you with great wealth because *you* wants to make you feel crappy about being poor?

What if *you* tells you to donate all of your assets to the Church of Scientology?

My dreams have let me down for as long as I can remember. They told me I could stuff a basketball when I couldn't.

They made me believe I was a genius, though I wasn't.

And three or four times they persuaded me I was a confidant of President Clinton—a dream job, to be sure. But how often must I rise to the pinnacle of success in my dreams?

Only to fall flat on my face in real life.

Enough already.

What purpose does it serve for my college sweetheart to break up with me for the hundred and sixtieth time?

How often must I get fired from the same job without getting severance pay?

God, if I had known I'd continue to be tortured by the Secret Service for counterfeiting when I was in college, I would have chosen a few years in prison instead.

Let me put this in simpler terms. Dreaming is no way to go through life.

They nearly convinced me that my wife was having an affair when she was parked safe at home.

They've introduced me to a fish called Tripe that wasn't even a fish when I ordered it for real.[2]

And they've given me delusions of grandeur.

I'm so much more interesting than that old Dos Equis guy, don't you think?

But now, perhaps because of the aging process…

Or my sleeping pills… Or the memory loss I'm experiencing… Or the medical marijuana I now enjoy…

I'm no longer under the inescapable influence of dreams.[3]

Only pipe dreams.

Like my quest to win a Nobel Prize in Literature.

Are you laughing with me? Or at me?

---

1. I believe my brain must have been mis-wired at birth. And that's why I refer to my writing in this chapter as a congenital disability.

2. Tripe is the meaty (sic) stomach wall lining of a cow. I haven't seen it on any menus since I ordered it at the Popponesset Inn on Cape Cod in 1978. Thankfully, it's now gone from theirs too.

3. Though I'm a professional daydreamer, I didn't dream up any of the dreams in this chapter. I really had them and have suffered greatly as a result. Though my wife might say she's the one who has suffered more from the errant punches I've thrown while asleep.

25

I performed the first "non-comedy" standup routine.
(How to make people laugh without being funny.)

I ONCE THOUGHT ABOUT being a stand-up comedian. And I might have been one if not for one little thing.

I'm not a funny guy.

Lighthearted?

For sure.

Somewhat humorous?

Perhaps.

But funny?

Seldom.

The honest truth is that my own kids used to call me Daddy Downer, though I'm convinced it was their damn shrink who put them up to it.

And my mother once called me the "death of the party." But that was at my son's Bar Mitzvah, right before the paramedics arrived.

Then there's my wife. She thinks my sense of humor makes no sense. That I speak in non-sequiturs.

But I ask you, am I alone in thinking science fiction will no longer exist in a thousand years? And if not, what will we all be reading then? Historical fiction? I find the very idea of historical fiction hysterical. But take it from me. I'm no judge of what's funny and what isn't.

However, that didn't stop little old contrarian me from putting together an act unlike all other acts ever created in the long history of laughter.

Instead of saying or doing funny things like comedians do, I decided to make audiences go gaga doing the polar opposite. I would make them laugh *without* using any humor whatsoever. The concept was a cosmic mindblower.

I had created a new performing art form—one I thought deserving of its own special category. I coined it "non-comedy." And with its advent, I became the world's first and only non-comedian.

If ever there was a man made for the times, it was me. That's because nobody was laughing at much of anything when I finished writing my act in the fall of '08. The financial meltdown had hit, unemployment had skyrocketed, the housing market had fallen apart, and the middle class had lost its retirement income.

People were in despair.

This, of course, made me happy, because non-comedy just happens to be the perfect vehicle for delivering bad news.

Something I'm quite good at by the way.[1]

I knew if I could make this downtrodden audience laugh at the horrors of life, I'd be on the cutting edge of non-comedy. Fame and fortune would soon be mine. But first I had to put my act into action.

The plan? Start by going to a comedy club to learn the ropes, then embark on a full non-comedy tour in Baltimore, Buffalo, Detroit, Cleveland, Milwaukee and Newark. The poor, depressed souls in those poor, depressed cities had so little to laugh about that I figured performing there would be a breeze.

Like, what could hecklers possibly say that might rattle me? Tell me that I suck? I already know I suck. Sorry, but to get under my skin, they'd have

127

to scream out the worst thing you can ever say to a non-comedian.

"You're *effin'* hilarious."

But that wasn't about to happen since I never took my show on the road.[2] After running it past my wife, she discouraged me from heading to Flint, Michigan, to hone my craft. But in fairness to me, that was because she didn't quite understand what non-comedy was about.

I repeat: The purpose of non-comedy is to make people laugh without saying or doing anything funny, like this oh-so-tragic affair.

A laughing hyena was run over by a car this morning in Little Rock, Arkansas. The last word it uttered was *ha*.

Like all non-comedians—again, namely me—there was a time when I was encouraged to try my hand at regular comedy. It happened at the University of Illinois in 1970 after a campus cop caught me urinating in an alley.

"What are you? Some kind of comedian," he said.

Though I believed my whole life had been a bad joke up to that time, I found his words encouraging. I asked if he thought I might become one for real. Know what he did? He laughed at me. Derisively.

It was neither the first nor last time I had been an object of ridicule.

People have always made me the butt of the joke. But that's to be expected, given my background. I used to be a traveling salesman. Married twice. The second time to a farmer's daughter.

Before that, I was a rabbi, always walking into bars for no apparent reason.

And many, many years ago, I was an electrician's apprentice.[3] But for some inexplicable reason, I could never screw in a light bulb by myself.

With a résumé like that, I knew it was best to avoid traditional comedy. Yet my gut kept telling me I had what it takes to make people roll in the aisles. Without saying or doing anything funny, that is. A mere amateur might be hard-pressed to accomplish that. But unfunny humor comes naturally to me. For instance...

I can make you break out in nervous laughter in a nanosecond, just by pulling down my pants and showing you a septuagenarian anus.

Or I can make you die laughing, like the CIA does when they tickle terrorists to death.

Or I can make you laugh and cry at the same time by slamming your funny bone on a table.

Or I can make you laugh at the misfortune of others, like when your boss dies in a car accident the same morning he was going to fire you.

Or I can make you laugh until you're sick, and then give you the best medicine for it. More laughter because I'm plain sadistic.

Or I can make you laugh for no apparent reason. It's easy with laughing gas.

Or I can make you laugh on the inside while you're crying on the outside, just like you did when your wealthy friend lost all his money in the stock market.

Thank you, thank you, a million times, thank you. But please hold all of your thunderous applause till the end of this chapter. It's throwing off my non-comic timing. Or better yet, please stop laughing altogether. Who needs you anyway? I know I don't. I travel with my own laughter.

Canned laughter!

Sorry, but non-comedy is too serious a business to be left to humor alone. With canned laughter in hand, I might one day rule the non-comedic world. Excuse me while I laugh insanely.

Ha, ha, ha, ha, ha...

I hate to be the bearer of bad news, but this morning a four-hundred-pound, western lowland gorilla slipped on a banana peel. Zoo goers were caught laughing at the scene.

Again, I ask, "Am I alone in thinking horrible news is funny?"

I think not.

A Wall Street banker was shot this morning at his new house. It was for a two-page spread in Architectural Digest.

And just last week, a doctor told me all signs point to cancer. But then I discovered he was reading my astrology chart.

Hey, you! Yeah, you, the person reading this page right now. Stop all your guffawing. Don't you know it's impolite to laugh at another person? It's not like I'm doing this act for laughs anyway. I'm doing it as a public service for all of my readers out there.

For those who were class clowns.

And that's all you were.

For those who were always made fun of.

But were never in on the joke.

And for those who think they're damn funny.

But never when people are around.

Again, thank you. A million times, thank you.

And have a fucking lousy night.

---

1. When a high school classmate's wife asked me if her husband and I had had a good time at our class reunion, I replied, "Oh, he went? I didn't see him there."

2. I performed my act in a speech class at Northwestern University. It brought down the house—*er*—classroom. Not one student, however, asked me for a signed eight-by-ten glossy. The next day I was a nobody once again.

3. If I had stayed on as an apprentice in 1971, I might have gone on to become a union electrician. But I quit after stepping on a hot wire that turned my long straight hair into a Jewfro. And that's why there's a dearth of straight-haired Jewish electricians today. (I told you I wasn't funny.)

26

I braved a night surrounded by wild animals.
(How to escape life's constraints and become one with nature.)

I DARED NOT fall asleep.

How could I? It was past midnight, and I was surrounded by dozens of wild creatures with nobody around to save me. I had to make it through the night. Just *had* to. If not for survival's sake, then for the sake of the story I was producing.

No, I wasn't on safari for the Today show.

I was locked inside the Lincoln Park Zoo in Chicago.

Well, not *locked.* I could have left at any time. But with the authority of NBC News behind me, I decided to spend the night. The folks running the zoo granted me full access.

I wish I could say I went for a noble cause, a "save the whale" sort of thing.[1] But my motivation for the outing was more personal. I wanted to study animal behavior in an unnatural habitat to see if there might exist a common ground between man and beast.

After all, they were all innocent animals who had been placed behind bars for doing nothing wrong, the same as I had been punished so many times before for things I never did. The information I might glean from such an (ad)venture, might be helpful to understanding human behavior as well.

131

Get off your high horse, Rick. You didn't even like any of the seven dogs you owned.

With little in the way of trepidation, I headed out into the solace of the night as one of the lucky few to discover what true zoo safariing was all about.

I write "lucky few" because two others tailed my every move if it became necessary to shoot the animals should they not be as sympathetic to my plight as I was to theirs. But they came unarmed. They were the cameraman and soundman.

And I was the walrus.

Goo goo g'joob.

Because, like Walruses, I can fall asleep on the spot.[2]

Most animals can't. They're light sleepers, incessantly keeping an eye out for nightmarish predators who would rip them to shreds if given half a chance. But I wondered, would that also hold true in a predator-free habitat like a zoo?

The only way to answer that question was to shadow these animals in the dead of night and find out for myself.

Would they prowl and growl?

Gnaw and claw?

Or simply snore and ignore?

Thanks to the knowledge I gleaned from my overnight stay, I can confirm that zoo animals are no different than their wilder brothers and sisters. They re-animate fast if you invade their space while asleep, much like extra-terrestrials would scare the living *nightlights* out of you if they snuck into your bedroom at three in the morning.

Excluding ET, of course, who had to be the most adorable alien in existence. Almost as cute as elephants, bears, chimps, and apes appear to be in the daytime when visitors safely enter the front gate.

But after sundown, watch out! Even a jovial elephant is known to voice its displeasure when human footsteps approach in the night.

"Shush. Can't an elephant get any sleep around here?"

And sleepy lions are prone to lyin' if a Great White News Hunter strays too close in the wee morning hours.

"Come a little closer, you dumbbell. That's right. Don't worry. I won't bite. Promise."

But giraffes, not known for vocalizations of any kind, have little to say when aroused from the five-minute naps they catch while standing on all fours. They're pretty much thunderstruck when you tippy-toe past them.

"   *," is what one giraffe told me.*

Of course, I'm making this entire talking animal schtick up. You do understand that, right? But it did seem like a pretty good pretense for interviewing the zoo's residents to see what they were up to when all the paying customers were gone. I mean, who better to tell us about their late-night shenanigans than the animals themselves?

You might find this a little strange, (or maybe not, now that you know me better). But I've conducted many weird interviews in my life.

And it wouldn't be the first-time critters spoke. The personification of animals has been a frequent device in TV-land. But has never been used in news features because news isn't news when talking animals have a say.[3]

I don't know why I feel it necessary to break new ground in all the endeavors I undertake, I just do. Whenever I confront a norm, I automatically seek out the abnormal. And, in this case, I wasn't about to let an opportunity to humor an audience slip away.

Even if it was for the news.

So, when I asked the zookeeper if I could talk to a few of the zoo's creatures, she predictably snickered as she replied, "This is for the news?"

I promised her it was.

Then, "Be my guest," she said.

When she learned I'd be sticking a boom mic in their faces, however, she nixed the whole *Dr. Dolittle* act. Said it would spook the animals. But that was because she didn't know I had a special way with animals—many of them being mammals like me.

In my opinion, they were practically family, significantly reducing the chances of any of my thirty-millionth cousins[4] going apeshit on me.

But I wasn't about to test the zookeeper's patience at such a late hour. I agreed to keep the microphone—and myself—well outside the cages, and proceeded to interview some of the zoo animals with caution.

It's not easy to get animals to talk, but it helps if you speak their native language. I happen to speak multiple animal tongues.

As a point of fact, I once convinced a bunch of cows in a pasture to come and talk to me—and boy, did they come running. But I can't take too much credit for them heeding my request for a visit. It was a skill I had picked up while covering a "Cow Calling" contest in Miami, Texas.

However, getting a positive response from country cows doesn't count for much. Since they're domesticated farm animals, it's far easier to speak to them than animals of the wild or their zoo ilk.

But it also helps that I have a special gift for interviewing inanimate objects, such as the sit-down interview I conducted with a *Man on A Bench* on the Illinois Institute of Technology campus. He refused to answer any of my questions.

That's always iffy when you interview statues.

Also, I once questioned marks for A.C. Nielsen. But every question I asked was followed by another question mark.

I have no idea why. Do you?

And then there was the set of World Book Encyclopedias I once quizzed on a variety of subjects. I found each of the volumes annoying.

They were a bunch of know-it-alls.

But none of this has anything to do with the night I spent in a zoo. Truth is, little of interest happened there, other than an imagination gone amok. Maybe Paul Simon was wrong when he sang.

"It's all happening at the zoo."

And maybe people's lives, mine included, sometimes seem more attractive than they really are. Still, I had a gas.

Hey, did somebody just cut one?

I'll let Jane answer that.

———————————

1. I started a "Save The Collie" movement after producing a feature story on modern dogs—and all the new designer breeds popping up. I thought they might lead to the extinction of Collies. Don't believe me? Then ask yourself when was the last time you saw one. Reruns of *Lassie* don't count.

2. I take Trazodone to help me sleep. It takes less than five minutes to work. And its only adverse side effect is suicide. I can live with that.

3. I produced fake news stories for corporate clients long before *fake news* was in vogue. They were called video news releases, VNR's for short. These deceptive news packages were indistinguishable from legitimate news stories. Hundreds floated in and out of newsrooms when I was in the business. On slow news days, most news directors filled open time slots in their programs with these phony-baloney pieces. They were the mainstay of my business until 2007. That's when the FCC concluded newsrooms were defrauding viewers by airing these stories as actual news. They began to crack down on stations that didn't identify them as paid advertisements. I'm happy to report that I no longer mislead the people of these United States. I leave that to politicians, social media platforms, and movies based on alleged actual events.

4. The rise of mammals on this planet started about two hundred million years ago. Since the vast majority of them reproduced anywhere from a few months old to fifteen years of age, a paleontologist might suggest that there's been on average about thirty million generations of mammals on Earth. That's the figure I used above in referencing my thirty-millionth cousins.

27

I could have blown the Today show off the air.
(How to be trustworthy when the majority of the world's not.)

JANE PAULEY OF THE *Today* show once wrote this about me.

"Who the hell was that guy? He brought out the best in me."

She sent that flattering comment in an email to my then partner Mike Leonard, a feature correspondent on the show. It came the day after I had interviewed Pauley, along with all the major on-air *Today* show talents, for a story set to air during the show's upcoming trip on the Orient Express in the late eighties.

Working out of the Chicago bureau, I had never met anyone on the show before. And it was nice to know I had made a good first impression with one of the "biggies" in New York.

It also confirmed how capable of an interviewer I could be.

For some reason unbeknownst to me, I had a knack for making people feel super comfortable in my presence. So comfortable they'd share their innermost thoughts, continuously blabbing away about things they'd never otherwise part with.

If I could interview myself, I'd probably admit that I shower naked.

It's fair to write that my skillset was the perfect one for a news producer. However, I'm quite sure I could have been a first-rate hairdresser if I had been inclined, happily lending a supportive ear to my female clients' indiscretions.

"What was your husband's reaction when he saw you kissing the plumber through the window?"

Or perhaps I could have been a top-notch psychiatrist, thoughtfully zeroing in on the cause of my patients' mental maladies.

"Can you tell me why you need me to tell you why you feel the way you do?"

Or maybe I could have been a highly decorated detective, entrapping suspects unaware that they had been outwitted.

"So after Easter came and went, Mr. Dahmer,[1] *Why'd you continue to skin live bunny rabbits?"*

Yes, that's what I was. Half detective, half producer.

It was the perfect role for me to play when I grilled the show's on-air talents about the crime caper soon to unfold on their train ride to Istanbul. It was going to be a murder mystery. Somebody on the show was going to kill Mike's story. And it was up to me to find out *whodunit* before the fact, allowing Mike to include it in the storyline. The motive for the murder was going to be airtime.

Whoever killed the story would be gaining precious on-air minutes of his—or her—own.

I gathered all the usual suspects and sat them down in their respective offices in New York. One by one, I got them talking about the make-believe murder. Until I got the truth out of all of them.

Too much truth as it turned out.

As the camera rolled, the stars of the show began to divulge all their dirty laundry. They shared unsolicited grievances and petty jealousies, (excluding Ms. Pauley, who was delighted by her performance.)

And they bitched and carped and kvetched about one another.[2]

At first, I thought they were all joking. But it slowly dawned on me that I was being let in on a *hush-hush* inside secret. The *Today* show was not one big happy family as portrayed on television.

It was a sham, as the following subplot illustrates.

Bryant and Willard disliked each other with a passion. Bryant considered Willard an air hog and wanted him off the show. But he couldn't get rid of him because Willard was the darling of senior citizens, a TV audience which kept his Q-score high[3]—and the show's ratings even higher. Willard was well aware that his elderly fanbase protected him from the wrath of Gumbel—and the door. And he played up to his audience every chance he could.

And you, silly centenarian, believed Willard's hundredth birthday wishes were from the bottom of his heart.

It would have blown the show off the air if America had known the truth. I had it all on four bombshell tapes. On my flight back to Chicago, I held onto the cassettes like my life depended on it.

Nonetheless, as I'm prone to do in the long silences of redeye flights, I drifted off into nothingness—the final stage of pre-sleep, only to be jolted back to reality by a dangerous thought.

Temptation.

Damn temptation can destroy marriages.

Lead to a life of crime.

Or result in suicide.

And that's just in my life. In yours, it might lead to one more potato chip, an unwanted pregnancy, or a late-night text to a married former lover.

But make no mistake. It was temptation that stirred up a thought that I wouldn't have had if not for the tapes clutched in my hands.

They made me think about the million dollars I could get from the

National Enquirer. Or from one of the other half-dozen rags that would have loved to expose the truth about the show.

Oddly enough, Steve Friedman, the executive producer of the show, had reached a similar conclusion at the same moment I had. He realized the show was vulnerable to the uncontrollable impulses of one Rick Leslie—a virtual nobody in the scheme of things. And Friedman wasn't about to let any peon like me destroy his career.

The next morning, he called up our office in Chicago and demanded the tapes back. Pronto.

I overnighted them that afternoon.

Though I was hurt that Friedman didn't trust me implicitly, he was right to ask for the tapes. I couldn't be trusted. Nobody can when it comes to money, work, love, or other personal matters. Somebody out there will always come along and snatch everything you have if you're not careful.

I once asked a college friend of mine to walk my girlfriend to class for me. I never saw her again.

Sadly, there is no shortage of untrustworthy jerks in this world. Sometimes I wonder why I'm not one.

I mean, I'm sure you'll think I am.

After what I did next.

---

1. Three years later, I produced a story on Jeffrey Dahmer for ABC World News Tonight. If I had had the opportunity to interview him, I wouldn't have had the nerve to ask him the bunny question I wrote in this chapter in jest. Or should I type *ingest*.

2. After I left the *Today* show, Bryant Gumbel wrote an internal memo saying much the same thing as he had said on my tapes. After it was leaked to the press, it marked the beginning of the end for *Today's* well-protected guardianship of morning television.

3. In the TV biz, the Q-rating measures the likability factor of celebrities. The higher their score, the greater their appeal to the viewing public.

28

I pissed in some guy's bottle of Pepto Bismol.
(How to protect yourself from someone like me.)

HOW CAN I PUT this gently? *This* not being an easy thing to admit. But I promised you juicy details at the start of this book, and believe me, my life never got any juicier than this.

I once pissed in some guy's bottle of Pepto Bismol.

If that makes me a jerk, so be it. Though I think prick might be a more appropriate term given the circumcision—err—circumstances. But there's really no logical reason for you to recoil from such a distasteful act. It's not like you haven't heard of crap like this cropping up before.

Example:

In the film *The Help*, a cleaning lady thanked her employer for treating her like a slave by baking the bitch a batch of brownies cooked up with you-know-what.

Audiences cheered during that scene. And everyone knows, including you, that crap is far worse than piss.

In that light, it's not really fair to judge me harshly. Besides, the guy whose bottle I had pissed in had it coming. It was his fault that he had never learned the moral of this story, best described by this old Yiddish proverb.

Ton nit khrap in de zelbe top ir kokhn in.

In English, that loosely translates to "never crap in the same pot you

140

cook in." In terms of everyday life, it also means you should never treat waiters or busboys like dirt when dining in their restaurants, never give another driver the finger when he or she lives down the block from you, and never pull any other crap on anyone able to crap all too easily over you.

What I find strange about this moral is that it even exists, proving that vengeance shitting and pissing must have occurred a lot throughout human history. In response to that, I say, "You got to get even somehow."

However, I never would have stooped to such gross misbehavior myself if not for a C-list celebrity named Merle. I won't share his last name with you, but he was affectionately called "The Butcher" due to his syndicated column in Thursday newspaper food sections everywhere. In real life, Merle was anything but kind.

When I met him in the early nineties, while producing a corporate video for Ziploc Freezer Bags up in Marin County, California, he was a bitter, middle-aged man who felt he deserved to be a big star. But like most minor celebs, he lacked the talent to back it up.

For reasons I'll soon get to, Merle took all his anger and frustrations out on me on the first day of the shoot, hurling an onslaught of slurs and slights in my direction. Being the upstanding citizen that I am, I was able to cast his aspersions aside.

Who am I kidding? I could never do that.

The real reason why I didn't respond to Merle's insults was that I couldn't. He was the spokesperson in the video. If he had walked off the set, I'd be the one paying the piper—the cost of the full production.

But Merle couldn't leave well enough alone. He had to cross the line between *ass* and *hole* by calling me an "incompetent boob." Now if he had said this to my face, I might have dressed him down and left it at that.

But no. "The Butcher" said this to my client, while I stood just ten feet away, as if I was the invisible man. There I stood. Totally pissed off but unable to do much about it. The client's PR woman, well aware of what was going on, walked over to check on me.

"Are you all right," she asked?

Though sympathetic to my plight, she tried to justify Merle's conduct by letting me know he wasn't just the on-camera talent, but also the former executive producer of all of Ziploc's prior corporate videos before I had supplanted him.

In effect, I had taken money out of "The Butcher's" own apron pockets, and drained him of the prestige of being the top dog, effectively turning him into a sworn enemy.

""""

Those aren't typos above. They're the world's smallest tears.

Showing little in the way of sympathy, I told her I still wanted to punch the guy out. Alarmed, she issued the following warning. "If you do that, we'll have to sue you."

Powerless to fight back, the shoot continued with Merle flinging vicious barb after barb at me. I took the beating like a non-violent Hindu monk. Until an old Jewish proverb began repeating itself in my head.

Ton nit khrap in de zelbe top ir kokhn in.

Yes, this butcher had committed a major boo-boo. He had crapped in the same pot he had cooked in by using his own kitchen as the film set. Thereby squeezing a nice location fee out of my budget, without realizing he was also opening up the door to my sweet—yet acidic—revenge by doing so.

I found that door at the threshold of Merle's bathroom after the shoot wrapped the following day. My bladder full from all the coffee and diet cokes I had drunk during a long, ten-hour shoot. I went in to take a leak.

That's when I noticed the medicine cabinet off to the right. I approached it curiously. No, not curiously. Suspiciously. Merle might have rigged the inside with loose marbles to sound the alarm if someone opened it and invaded his privacy.

Should I or shouldn't I, I debated internally.

It was an easy decision. I stopped urinating midstream. (That's my way of writing that I opened the cabinet with extreme caution.) I heard no marbles rattling inside, so I swung the door open and saw an unmistakable flash of pink. I recognized what it was immediately—a bottle of Pepto Bismol. It was proof positive that "The Butcher" suffered from a very delicate stomach condition.

"Take me," it shouted.

Virtually on cue, imaginary music swelled up in a Muslim call to prayer. *Hayya 'ala-s-Salah. Hayya 'ala-s-Salah. Hayya 'ala-s-Salah. Hayya 'ala...*

It was then that I realized revenge wasn't a dish best served cold. It was better served hot, like body temperature hot. I reached for the bottle, unscrewed the cap, and in sibilant silence—*ssss*—squirted a short stream of warm liquide gold into it.

Take a swig of this, you bastard.

Granted, it was Pepto Abysmal behavior on my part. I was fairly certain, though, I wasn't a psychopathic urinator, having never gone further than whizzing in parking lots, pools, showers and alleys before.

And maybe scriptwriting in virgin snow a dozen times or so.

And maybe, just maybe, one kitchen sink.

But the important thing to know is that I've never made it a habit to fool others into drinking my urine.

In Merle's case, however, there was a principle involved. If you don't treat the people around you respectfully, you can't expect to be treated respectfully yourself.

Though an eye for an eye is not a commandment I adhere to...

Commandments five through ten are okay, but the first four have to go.

...and though I don't believe the ends justify the means in all cases...

Unless the means are due to meanness.

...I do believe in equal justice under the law.

Especially for me.

With that in mind, Merle got what he deserved. I don't think it would have done much good if I had sent him ten useless magazine subscriptions? Or teepeed his house with two-ply tissue? The punishment wouldn't have fit the crime.

But a few drops of drinkable, kidney-filtered urine for someone as big a schmuck as Merle had been most certainly did.

In Yiddish, dear Christian and Muslim readers, a schmuck, quite appropriately, is a penis.

I didn't hear or even think about "The Butcher" again for the next ten years. Then one day I bumped into Ziploc's PR woman on the street. As we reminisced about old times, she brought up the subject of Merle. She asked if I knew what had happened to him. I couldn't have cared less, but she shared the news with me anyway.

"Merle died from ulcerative colitis a few years ago."

I don't believe my urine had anything to do with Merle's guts imploding. A far more plausible explanation would have been the burning and persistent anguish he must have felt when he discovered the video that I had produced wound up in three thousand new refrigerators and freezers in appliance stores everywhere.

And that I had netted three bucks a copy.

But that's chump change compared to what I made at McDonald's.

29

I made almost $1,000 an hour at McDonald's.
(How to make a financial killing on a minimum wage salary.)

MY ADVICE TO YOU, if you own or manage a business, is to never hire someone like me.

McDonald's made that mistake when they first brought me on as its *fry guy* and *shake maker* in 1971. It was my first job after college, not quite a stellar start to my daydreaming career to come.

But I had always loved Mickey D's from the first time I went there in 1955. The wafting aroma of their burgers would drive me bonkers every time my parents drove past their lone location in a nearby Chicago suburb. So working at McDonald's part-time during the day seemed like a good idea while I performed nights in Lincoln Park's music scene in 1971.

At that time, McDonald's paid the minimum wage—a buck sixty—with no complaints from me. By the time I was fired later that first day, I had earned a whopping six dollars and forty cents for my efforts.

Not too shabby for four hours of work.

I'm sure the restaurant manager (also named Rick) was glad to see me exit the premises as well. I know for a fact that he hoped to never see me again. As things turned out, he didn't. Though I believe he would have preferred future get-togethers if he had had the prerogative.

But that was well after the accident—my accident. Not the other *Rick's*.

It went down this way. I had gone down to McDonald's basement to get a fifty-pound sack of potatoes, but found it stacked high atop other bags on the shelf, mere inches beyond my reach. I stood on my tippy-toes and slid the sack out a bit to get a firmer grip. But with my arms fully extended, it was still too awkward to lift. So I took a half-step back for better support.

Unaware that a sump pump basin lay behind

me.

(Ow!!!)

Above is a visual depiction of how my left leg dropped down the well when the pump's flimsy cover gave way under my two hundred pounds of pressure, causing my testicles to slam onto the concrete floor.

Nobody saw it happen.

Nobody heard it happen.

But it just so happened that Manager Rick was coming down the stairs seconds after. He found me screeching. Half above ground, half below.

He was wise to the ways of troublemakers, (though I wasn't one). But he had little experience with born smilers like me. (My constant smile makes me look guilty even when I'm not.)

It resulted in *Rick* accusing me of staging the entire incident. (I swear I didn't.) And then he fired me on the spot. But it wasn't the shortest job I ever held. That record belonged to Sears and me. I had worked there for forty-five minutes when I was nineteen.[1]

However, my four hours at McDonald's did turn out to be one of my most rewarding jobs. That's because I hadn't learned to despise lawyers yet. I spoke to one the next day.

He said, "You shouldn't let guilty corporations get away with murder."

I wanted to add, "Or sore balls." But didn't. Even at twenty-three I knew it was inappropriate language to use around scholars and professional people.

Excluding physicians, of course, who hear stuff like that all the time.

And by readers who say they're disgusted by toilet humor but really aren't.

But that has nothing to do with the story. Other than the fact that the day after I injured my testicles, we lodged an official complaint against McDonald's for non-compliance of Illinois labor laws.

The Illinois Labor Relations Board heard the case. It was *Rick's* word against mine—a stalemate between opposing statements. The case was about to be thrown out when I got word from my lawyer that something weird had occurred. *Rick* had been in a terrible car accident, and was—in both police and emergency room parlance—DOA.

Gee, what are the odds of two Poor Ricks in one book. (See Chapter 7 song lyrics)

Of course, I felt sorry for the guy. He didn't deserve to die for calling me a liar when he was the one who lied.

But without his testimony, I was awarded six dollars and forty cents in back pay.

Plus, another sixteen hundred for pain and suffering.

Or about four hundred dollars an hour—just about what a good lawyer made in those days.

My attorney said nothing like that had happened to him before. He asked if I had some mystical ability that I had used to kill my accuser, and wanted to know if it was safe to send me a bill. I'm sure he was kidding. But that was when I first became aware that good things happened to those who liked me.

And bad things happened to those who didn't.

By way of example, the guy who kicked me out of my high school band deserved the punishment he had coming. He became a doctor with exorbitant malpractice insurance.

He must have suffered horribly, whereas I led a debt-free life.

But again, that has nothing to do with the story. Other than my financial future took another good turn two years later when McDonald's unknowingly contracted me to sing on one of their TV commercials. During the recording session, I was tempted to tell their marketing manager about my past earnings from McDonald's, but thought it best to remain silent. I didn't want it on my conscience in case the elevator down the hall dropped six stories to the ground floor with him on it.

Please tell me it's normal to fantasize about stuff like this.

I came back to reality seconds later, and sang a few *mi-mi-ma-mo-mu* vocal exercises to get my voice in shape for the four-part harmony jingle I was about to sing. Giving it my all, I belted out...

"You deserve a break today at McDonald's."

The spot aired nationally.

After the first thirteen weeks of play, the typical broadcast cycle for commercials, I received a royalty check for over thirty-three hundred dollars, hardly a paltry payday for an hour's work. It was enough to get me daydreaming about a new jingle-singing career.

Unfortunately, after that cycle ended, McDonald's shifted gears and switched ad campaigns. Their new tagline?

"We do it all for you."

I smile at that theme line now because McDonald's had indeed done it *all* for me. In total, they had paid me $4,906.40 for five hours of work. That works out to about a thousand dollars an hour—my highest hourly wage ever. With that kind of money, you can buy an awful lot of those incredible tasting McDonald's burgers I mentioned upfront.

Regrettably, you can't find them anymore. No matter how hard you look. That's because McDonald's doesn't cook their burgers the same way they used to. If I cared more—or owned stock in the company—I'd let its CEO know where Mickey D's went wrong.

But I'm more interested in the days when my own life could have gone wrong.

But didn't.

Fifth grade was that tough.

---

1. I worked in shipping and receiving at Sears. My job was to stamp the price on the river of goods that flowed past me on the conveyer belt. I tried keeping up with the line like Lucy Ricardo tried when she worked at the chocolate candy factory in season two, episode one of *I Love Lucy*. But it was hopeless. When the line stopped momentarily, I thought half the day had gone by, but the clock said different. It had only been 45 minutes. I snuck out the back door without getting paid.

30

I was bullied by my fifth-grade teacher.
(How to shape a better future through adversities of the past.)

I AM MICKEY MANTLE, switch-hitting slugger of the New York Yankees. Ripper of rawhides, launcher of long balls. Young boys idolize me for the tape measure home runs I hit. Pretty girls eye me as I round the bases.

I am ten years old. A fourth-grade hero on his way to becoming a fifth-grade hero. Or so I think. Until the eighth of September, 1958. The first day of school. And she is nowhere to be found.

She is Mrs. Wallach, my new teacher—the one every fifth-grade kid was hoping to get. She is kind, sweet, and nurturing. But she is also pregnant and has stopped teaching. In her place stands a broad-shouldered man. He's not the kind of teacher one might expect to teach innocent ten-year-old children.

Over the ensuing months, the person known as me will cease to exist. I will be erased like chalk on a blackboard. For years, I will dream of vengeance for the harm he inflicts on me.

His name is Sergeant Zweitz, as in *hates*. That's right, he calls himself Sergeant, and appropriately so, for he will run fifth grade like the platoons he drilled in the Marine Corps.

At recess that first day, the boys play baseball as usual. But the topic of conversation is less about batting averages—and more about Zweitz. I can't help but make fun of his name like you might expect a ten-year-old to do. It reminds me of Zwieback. That makes the other kids laugh. So does Major Trouble, Private Parts and Corporal Punishment.

But I'm the one who's about to be toast when I turn and see Zweitz standing beside me, his legs spread-eagled shoulder-length apart in a stance summoned up from his drill-instructing Marine Corps days.

"Recess is over for you," he barks.

He grabs me by the shirt collar, marches me back to the classroom, and leads me down the aisle to the last desk in the back row. There, he slams down my notebook, rotates the desk till it faces the back wall, and slides it into the corner. That will be my seat for the rest of the semester.

Every morning when I come into the classroom, Sergeant Zweitz will say, "Ricky, go to your corner."

After every recess. "Go to your corner."

His words will echo in my head for years.

Go.

To.

Your.

Corner.

This is nothing to smile about. But the harder I try not to grin, the wider my smile grows.

Do I go to the principal's office to complain?

No.

Do I clue my parents in on what is going on?

No.

I just continue to hide behind my cheerful mask and laugh in all the right places, swearing to one day avenge my tormentor. But what chance does a ten-year-old boy have against a grown-up bully? The correct answer to that rhetorical question isn't none. There is one place I can go—and do go—to escape.

My corner.

It's where my mind is free to travel to far-off places, free to discover unknown pathways worthy of exploration, and free to dream and question and wonder.

Do bees ever stop buzzing? What are fingernails made of? Does anyone really like Neapolitan ice cream?

Gee, I really was an imaginative little boy.

One day, I get so lost in my daydreams that I create a melody in my head. In a lapse of consciousness, I hum it aloud, unaware that the class has gone dead silent behind me.

The music, with no other commotion to absorb the sound, suddenly sweeps across the room. Though I'm lost in my own little world, I can tell something is off. I stop humming, swing around in my seat, and catch everybody staring at me.

A burst of laughter rises up throughout the classroom.

I'm totally embarrassed, but I need to somehow save face. I do the one thing that comes to mind. I stand up and take a bow.

I'd like to thank all of you boys and girls for being such an appreciative audience.

The laughter I get from the other kids turns the moment in my favor, but it has the opposite effect on Zweitz. He orders me out to the hall.

What follows next is pure hell.

He chides me. Teases me. Takes away my recess. Even puts me in a headlock. When nobody else is looking, his stupid smiles morph into sneers.

I hate him!

I hate him!!

I hate him!!!

As the leaves fall, my grades fall; as autumn retreats, I retreat. I turn from extrovert to introvert. From shining star to diminished candle. Would anybody be surprised if I grew up to be a serial killer?

Instead, I become a killer of cereal, devouring box after box of Frosted Flakes. They're grrreat! But they also add a little too much heft to my five-foot frame. With all that additional weight putting pressure on my knees, it soon hurts to walk downstairs at home, let alone run around the bases at school.

The doctor says I have *Osteochondritis Dissecans,* a bone disease more common to thoroughbreds than people. But it means the same thing for me as it does for those racehorses. My days as a stud are over.

I am no longer Mickey Mantle, switch-hitting slugger of the New York Yankees. Ripper of rawhides, launcher of long balls.

I am Rick Leslie. Imagineer of ideas, creator of melodies, dreamer of destinies.

I will one day grow up and perform my songs on stage. I will sing on commercials. I will go on to become an adman, a network news producer, a TV production company owner, a performing storyteller, and an author.

I will hit a few metaphorical tape-measure home runs down the road.

In a final act of revenge, I will one day chronicle the bullying I endured in fifth grade using Sergeant Zweitz's real name.[1] But by then, I won't be sure whether to kill him.

Or kiss him.

It wouldn't be the first time a guy tried to kiss another guy.

1. Thirty-some years ago, I learned from my children's babysitter that there was a teacher at a nearby junior high who had tormented one of his students, nearly driving the poor kid to suicide. The teacher turned out to be a Mr. Zweitz. Do you think he could have been related to Sergeant Zweitz?

31

I met a terrific guy on a train.
(How to survive a trip to hell—and live to write about it.)

I was having a beer when he put his arm around my shoulder, like he was a best buddy of mine. Then he leaned in for a kiss.

I froze.

Only then did I realize I had just had a serious lapse in judgement, but I didn't realize how serious until years later.

***

IF I WERE DIRECTOR Alfred Hitchcock, I'd call this chapter *A Stranger on A Train*.

But since I'm not prone to creating suspense beyond the suspense of the moment, I will share my story as it unfolded. In as much detail as I can recall.

Which is a great deal of detail. For memories of ominous intent are not soon forgotten. They stick with you forever, questioning your judgment and ability to see the world for what it truly is—a game of chance filled with unforeseen circumstances and unanticipated consequences for all the actions you choose, or do not choose, to take.

Little did I know that that was what I would soon be facing when I boarded the Illinois Central Panama Limited on my way back to college in Champaign, Illinois, in the fall of '67.

I grabbed a seat by the window, hoping some attractive girl would take the spot next to me. But as usual, she never came. (They never do).

Instead, some man who appeared middle-aged, but was maybe only five or six years older than me, grabbed the seat. He was an affable-looking fellow with a big smile—and an even bigger handshake.

"Hi, I'm John," he said.

I introduced myself and shook his hand with a firm grip and a hearty shake like my father had taught me. And that was that. Just two strangers brought together by fate, in a situation that plays out thousands of times a day on trains everywhere.

Over the next hour, we sat back in our seats, neither acknowledging the other. That's how subtle the seduction of nineteen-year-old Rick Leslie was going to be.

***

I threw his arm off my shoulder and backed away.

"Sorry, I'm not like that." I said, hoping that would be the end of it. But it wasn't.

"I just thought we'd have some fun." John said, mischievously.

***

"Kankakee, Illinois. Next stop, Kankakee"

The conductor's voice awakened me from a slumber precipitated by the wearying rumble of the train's rhythmic beating upon the tracks.

Ba-dum...Ba-dum...Ba-dum...

"You heading back to school?" John asked.

"Yeah."

"Whatcha taking?"

That little exchange initiated a conversation. First, small talk about college. Then more engaging topics like sports and politics. I learned John was temporarily staying in Urbana for a construction project he had contracted. I remember thinking I might get a good part-time job out of this. In those days, I was blind to the idea that a stranger might truly be strange.

***

How could I have been so stupid?

My mouth went dry, but I had to let John know in no uncertain terms that this wasn't going any further. However, the words I spoke came from the little boy I was at that moment.

"I want to go home."

***

Need I remind you that danger is all around us? It could be an air conditioner breaking loose from its window mountings as you walk past.

Or an evening stroll in the direction of muggers.

Or even a terrific guy on a train.

Menacing threats can dart into your life without warning., catching you off guard, and leaving you with split-second decisions to make.

Take a left and a bus hits you as you cross the street.

Hang a right and you live another day.

In less than an hour, the man sitting to my left would present me with one such decision while we whisked past acre after acre of corn bathed in the shadows of the colorless fall dusk.

***

John slowly inched forward, cornering me in his apartment.

"Oh God, please, no" were the words throbbing in my head. I had no idea who this guy was, or what he was capable of doing.

157

I felt like a woman about to scream at the top of her lungs.

***

"Champaign, Illinois. Next stop, Champaign."

The train rolled into the station. John and I said our pleasantries—nice talking to you and all—and went our separate ways. I jumped off the train and headed towards the baggage area, where I grabbed my suitcase and tried to hail a taxi back to campus.

And that is what would have occurred if not for the honk of a horn off to my right. I turned to see John pulling up to the curb in a big lavender convertible with its top down.

"Want a ride to campus?" He shouted.

A small alarm went off in my head. I chose to ignore it.

"Terrific," I yelled back, ignorant of the word's original root meaning— the creation of terror.

***

I saw a craziness in John's eyes that I hadn't noticed before. The phone rang. He ignored it.

"I can pay you," he said.

"No! I want to go."

"How 'bout you blow me first."

It wasn't a request.

***

John popped open his trunk. I tossed my suitcase in and hopped in the front. We pulled out and headed south towards campus, with the car radio blasting and the crisp fall air in our faces.

"Whaddaya say we get us some beers and a steak? My treat," he said.

A little voice inside me said *no*. But I said *yes* anyway. And with a quick spin of the wheel, we headed off to what I assumed would be one of the modest steakhouses near campus. In an attempt to act *cool*, I didn't say a word when we pulled up to a mid-rise apartment complex off in the boonies somewhere.

It was John's place.

You know those scenes in horror films where the teenager enters the house and the audience screams out in panic "Don't go in there. Are you crazy? Something bad is going to happen inside."

Well, you know how you don't believe that goes on in real-life.

You're wrong.

***

John stood between me and the door, blocking my way out of his apartment. Sensing real danger, I began to tremble, a sign that strength-inducing adrenaline was pumping into my system. Without thinking, I charged him like a raging bull, knocking him off balance, and ran out the door to freedom.

***

But I couldn't just run off. My suitcase was locked in John's trunk with my ID tag attached to the handle. I couldn't let it fall into his hands, so I stopped and turned around, finding John slumped in his doorway.

I shouted "Give me my suitcase now or I'm going to call the police."

"No-no-no-no police," he shot back staccato-like.

I warily backed off a safe distance as he hurried to his car and opened the trunk. I demanded he step away. Then I scurried up, grabbed my suitcase, and didn't look back. I hustled out of the subdivision and hitched a ride to campus.[1]

Back in the comforting womb of my apartment, I popped open a beer, sat back on the sofa, and dozed off to the sound of a train far off in the distance. I prayed it would carry that day far away.

And for a good while it did.

Twelve years, to be exact. That's when I saw John again. This time on TV. It was a mug shot. He had been accused of being a serial killer.

By all news accounts, John Wayne Gacy hadn't started killing when I met him. They say his first victim was murdered in 1972, five years after I stopped taking trains.

And two years before I started playing collegiate flag football.

---

1. If you're under the age of fifty, you might be wondering why I'd hop into another stranger's car minutes after my encounter with an even *stranger*. How dense can a kid be! However, I'm not sure I've learned my lesson yet. Just last week I went grocery shopping and bought some cream with an expired pull date. So it wouldn't be wrong of me to type that I'm still often dense. Worse yet, I still used that spoiled cream in my coffee.

32

I've got a politically correct n-word story to tell.
(How to learn life's lessons the hard way.)

"WHO YOU CALLING *n-word*, boy?"

His scowl made me want to *p*-word in my pants. But, in truth, I had said no such thing, having never used the *n-word* in my entire life. Nonetheless, his sudden accusation scared the *s-word* out of me.

"Answer me, *c-word*-sucker!" He went on.

I tried to speak, but my *d-worded* mouth went dry.

"You don't know *s-word* from Shinola, do you?" He said.

Before I could apologize to save my sorry *a-word*, his grimace broke into a wide, toothy grin.

"Sorry, man, I'm just *f-wording* around."

And that's how I met Eddie Russell, one of the most fun-loving mother-*f-worders* on the planet. It was at one *h-word* of a party on the University of Illinois campus during the *f-worded*-up hippie revolution.

It was an era that gave all students the freedom to become God-*d-worded* friends with anybody they wanted. Including someone who might not have been your friend a few years earlier.

Eddie was in no need of introduction to anybody on campus. He was the well-known all-conference, all-muscled offensive lineman on the Fightin' Illini team that had won the 1964 Rose Bowl. Russell played alongside future NFL Hall-of-Famer *D-word* Butkus.

After his final college season in 1966, Eddie was drafted by the Buffalo Bills of the newly-formed American Football League. Making the pros was a big *f-wording* deal, but Eddie had been assigned to the team's taxi squad whose roster consisted of players not quite good enough to suit up on Sundays.

That was where Eddie had lost his front tooth, leaving a gaping hole in his smile, perfect for sucking *p-wordy*, he would say.

As great a player as Eddie had been in college, Buffalo cut him after one season. With his glory days behind him, he returned to Champaign in the fall of '68. My buddies and I became friends with Eddie soon after. We'd *f-word* around on weekends, often getting *s-word*-faced at one of the half-dozen popular bars on campus.

It was my *f-wording* brilliant plan to add Eddie to our intramural flag football team. Maybe Eddie couldn't intimidate NFL linemen, but he sure as *h-word* could terrify any kid in our league. It surprised me when he agreed to play. For *C-word's*-sake, I thought, we were going to have a former pro football player on our side.[1]

Though we played just for fun, we were still out to win. And we knew with Eddie playing for us, victory was assured over a bunch of *p-wordy*-whipped frat boys. (Which is what I had been two years earlier before I quit fraternizing forever.)

Our next game was against Alpha Epsilon Pi the following Saturday morning. It was the official start of Parents Weekend, so a bigger crowd than usual would be on hand. Moms and dads, brothers and sisters would all be there.

We planned to keep Eddie under wraps until game time so everyone would be startled when we trotted out our intimidating six-foot-three, 260-pound, mother-*f-wording* ringer. But we had no clue that pro athletes also unnerved their opponents by employing every known swear word.

When the game began, Eddie didn't just kick *a-word*. He trash-talked his *a-word* off, embracing some of the filthiest *f-wording* language to come out of the NFL.

"Gonna squeeze your mama's t-wordies… Get ready to get your f-wording, a-word whipped, boy… Say bye-bye to your teeth, mother-f-worder… Ya know, your girlfriend b-worded-me last night…"

We were young. We were innocent. We should have known better. But we laughed our *a-words* off. Quite a few parents didn't find it funny, however. Some began to hiss and boo. And then rising above the din came a vulgar word that all decent folks know should never be uttered aloud, let alone to a black man.

"*N-word*, get your black *a-word* off the field," some old guy hollered.

A dark pall spread over the field.

There's no way for me to accurately depict what Eddie was feeling at that moment. In the vernacular of the times, it can only be described as a mother-*f-wording* bummer. The game came to a sudden halt, and both teams walked off, leaving Eddie standing alone at midfield. I headed over to him not knowing what to say, so I avoided the subject altogether.

I said, "Wanna grab a beer."

When I should have said.

I'm sorry I got you into this thing.

Eddie said, "Nah, I don't feel like it."

When he should have said:

This is the kind of bull-*s-word* I go through every day.

It would be the last time I saw Eddie. He left Champaign without saying goodbye. The following spring I saw a brief mention in the student newspaper about Eddie taking a coaching job at some high school up in northern Michigan.

As for me, it would still be years before I completely understood how crappy it was for a black person to live in a white world. Eddie had been right all along.

I didn't know shit from Shinola.

And Eddie became just one more person dropping out of my life too soon after dropping in.

Others would follow.

---

1. Even with a former pro football player on our side, we were losing the game when play stopped. *Let that teach you a lesson, Leslie.* It did.

33

I was a dear friend of Ernie Banks.
(How to convince others you're telling the truth when nobody believes you are.)

I GREW UP LIKING hall-of-fame shortstop Ernie Banks.

Little did I know that Ernie would one day like me. At least, that's what Ernie would say.

The first time I met Mr. Cub, he was swinging a club—a golf club. His baseball career a distant memory, Ernie could rocket a golf ball with the same break of his powerful wrists that once propelled baseballs out of Wrigley Field onto Waveland Avenue in Chicago.

"Fair ball," I yelled after Ernie had driven the ball about three hundred yards down the middle of the fairway.

Fair ball. Ernie liked that.

But I wasn't on the first tee to play a round of golf with the man. Or to flatter him, as the case may have been. I was there to profile Mr. Cub for *NBC Nightly News*. Over the course of four hours, I gathered B-roll footage of Ernie while interviewing him in various locations around the course and clubhouse.[1]

After our first meeting, Ernie called me his *dear friend* every time we were in each other's company, maybe four or five separate occasions over the following six years or so.

I always greeted him with my hand extended in friendship. But Ernie would have none of that formality. He'd grab my forearm instead and give it a hearty two-handed shake. Much more intimate than a routine handshake, it communicated a warmth that spoke of genuine interest.

I'm not sure Ernie did this with total sincerity, though. He seemed to treat everyone the same way, as if we were all someone of worthy prominence, deserving of his full attention.

Far more remarkable than that, Ernie never forgot anyone he met. Without fail, he could recall things you might have said to him in passing, and file it all away for another day's meet and greet.

It may be a bit of a stretch to call Ernie and me dear friends, considering we never went out for lunch, played poker, or saw a movie together.

I also didn't invite him to my son's bar mitzvah, but that might have been because my son Scott never attended Hebrew school. If he had, I might have sent Ernie an invite. And, being the kind of guy he was, he might have come. Without a doubt, that would have delighted Scott—a boy once nicknamed Cubby.

When Scott turned twelve, I told him I knew Ernie. Not yet appreciative of his dad's hobnobbing days with pro athletes and show biz celebs, Scott didn't believe me.

"C'mon, you're not friends with Ernie Banks," he'd say. "You're making it up."

His comment struck a nerve.

People have doubted my word for as long as I can remember. That includes my family who refuses to believe half the things I say, let alone all the stranger stuff that has happened to me.

Have I told you about the time I shared Thanksgiving with the Navajos? Or when I solved America's area code crisis? Or when I pissed next to President Ford? Or when

I made a fool of myself in front of Tom Brokaw? Or when a former Miss America invited me to her house for dinner? Or when I introduced Oprah to a national TV audience? Or when I beat up two fifth-graders in third grade? Or when I sparred with Muhammed Ali?

I don't know why so many question the veracity of my stories. Conceivably, it's because it defies explanation that so many strange happenings, weird thoughts, odd situations, wayward observations, and unfortunate misbehaviors could crop up in one person's lifetime.

Yet by examining myself in the third-person objective, I'm able to see how *Rick Leslie* might create a state of confusion in the minds of others.

"I know Rick claims he performed at the same club where John Prine became famous, but I never even heard him sing before. He must be lying."

And…

"Rick says he lied to his psychiatrist, but doesn't that defeat the whole purpose of getting help? He must be lying."

Or…

"How could Rick fondle a naked woman without touching her? That's impossible. He must be lying."

Or maybe I'm doubted because my whole persona suggests I'm a man of little gravitas. My good-natured, "gentle giant" demeanor sends an automatic instant message to others that I'm not telling the truth whenever I share the intimate moments of my life.

People! Let me shout it out so everybody can hear:

"I'M NOT MAKING ANY OF THIS SHIT UP."

Sure, I fudge some of the incidental details in my stories. But when you're leading a life of creative non-fiction like I am, it's okay to play a bit loose with the minutiae to help make a story work.

By that, I mean I'm a ninety-eight percent truth-teller.

That doesn't make me a liar. It makes me a writer. But that doesn't mean I like it when people don't believe what I'm telling them.

So how does all this relate back to my son?

Because five years after Scott claimed I was lying about Ernie, he discovered how honest his old man was. Simply by chance, he met Ernie Banks. Bumped into him at a Chicago Bulls game. Scott had left our nosebleed seats at halftime and gone down courtside where his friend had front row season tickets.

Something is wrong with the above picture. Me—the adult—seated high above the court. Scott—the child—seated down below.

If Scott hadn't deserted me for those better seats, though, he never would have seen Ernie sitting two rows behind. So near, so available, so welcoming that Scott just couldn't let an opportunity like that go to waste. He worked up his nerve and approached Ernie to see if his dad knew Ernie Banks for real, and wasn't the big fat liar he considered me to be. Was our relationship at stake? Only if Ernie's memory failed him.

Scott, who often shares this story with friends and business associates, says his brief conversation with Ernie went something like this.

"Excuse me, Mr. Banks. My dad says he's a friend of yours."

"Well, son," Ernie replied. "That would depend on who your father is. What's his name?"

"Rick Leslie, sir."

"Rick? Yeah, I know Rick," says Ernie. "He's a dear friend of mine. Is he here with you?"

Scott pointed to the rafters across the arena. "Uh, my dad's sitting up there."

"You must be Cubby then," Ernie said.

"Well, yeah. How do you know that?" Asked Scott.

Now, what an endearing story this would have been if Ernie had indeed referred to my son as Cubby—something he could have done because I had mentioned it to Ernie years earlier.

But Banks didn't say what I just said he did. That's the two percent of lies I put into every story. Of course, I just self-corrected this one. But that little fib wasn't needed to make this story work anyway. The rest of Scott and Ernie's conversation works fine without it.

"Say hello to your dad for me, will you?" Ernie *really* said.

"Sure, Mr. Banks, I will." Scott *actually* said.

And that's what Scott did when he returned to our nosebleed seats in the third quarter.

"Dad, I just met Ernie Banks down there. He called you a dear friend of his."

"Oh, really," I said, trying to hold back a smile that desperately wanted out.

Let the record show that Scott never doubted me again. Neither has my other son Jamie or daughter Alison. Frankly, I'm lucky to be their dad.

But sometimes I wonder if pure luck alone has anything to do with a person's good fortune.

---

1. Ernie was joined on the fairways by his former teammate, Billy Williams, who provided additional insights into Banks' background, demeanor and career.

34

I am an Agent of Fortune.
(How to make things better for everyone but yourself.)

DON'T BE MISLED BY my chapter heading. I've never made anyone rich.

But I have enriched their existence. Which may—or may not—result in financial gain. But as we all know, there's so much more to life than money. For example, there's your life's calling. That's where I come in if you're ever fortunate enough to meet me.

Rick, you're bragging. Stop it.

Okay, let's just say I enjoy helping people. Mainly young adults looking for the best direction to take through life's journey. I'm pretty good at guiding them down the right path. That's because I've been blessed with the power to change lives for the better.

Sometimes inadvertently, other times indirectly.

This power of mine isn't mystical, spiritual, or magical in nature. It's just who I am. For as long as I can remember, I've helped choreograph people's futures. And led them to their fortunes.

I know it sounds delusional to believe I hold such sway over young minds. But I assure you, I've got both feet planted firmly on the ground, except when my ego gets the best of me—an infrequent occurrence since I suffer from low self-esteem like perhaps seven or eight billion other humans do.

However, at this very minute, my confidence is riding high because I'm proud of the previous sentence I wrote.

I don't know why. I just am. Maybe it's because I had the guts to admit the unvarnished truth about myself.

So allow me a little leeway while I describe all the things I can accomplish—all exaggerations notwithstanding.

I'm a booster shot that boosts egos, because others can't believe in you until you believe in yourself.

But I'm even more than that.

I'm a therapist, a motivational speaker, and a life coach rolled into one, always looking for ways to push you forward.

But again, I'm way more than that.

I'm Prozac for the soul, constantly lifting your spirits and making you feel good about yourself.

No, I'm even more than that.

What I am is a Muse. Except there's no such thing as a male Muse. All Muses are in fact women. A man doing what I do has his own distinctive classification.

He's an Agent of Fortune.

As stated in the Urban Dictionary, an Agent of Fortune "*influences* and *inspires* other people to make decisions beneficial to their future." I meet those criteria. I'm not a figment of anybody's imagination, (other than my own). I really do exist, as do my beneficiaries.

But there is a downside to the life of an AOF. That being this: I'm unable to do for myself what I can do for you.

I'm directionless.

Rudderless.

Bouncing from path

to

path

to

path.

You can add three more "paths" to that list. (My resume is proof of that.)

Believe me, it sucks that I'm forced to sacrifice myself for the betterment of others. (I didn't volunteer for the job, I was just handed it at birth.) I take my special ability seriously, though.

Let me provide you with an example of how I changed one man's life for the better.

Mark Ringel was a junior high classmate of mine. At a class reunion many years after, he credited me with providing the impetus he needed to become a physician. Evidently, I had said something to him as a kid that had stuck with him his entire life, though I didn't learn about it until Marc was thirty-eight or thereabouts.

I had somehow *influenced* and *inspired* him when he lagged behind all the other eighth-grade boys running a mile in gym class. Poor Marc was huffing and puffing, about to give up, when I fell back alongside him. He said he couldn't make it. I said he could—and started encouraging him as we ran.

The words I spoke helped take Marc's mind off the task at hand, and he soon forgot about his shortness of breath and wound up finishing the race.

I was Marc's Agent of Fortune. I had bettered his future.

Even with many other credible witnesses supporting my claim, I recognize many of you may be doubting my typewritten word right now.

You may not believe that Agents of Fortune exist. For you, I provide another possible explanation for the powers I hold.

I might just be a Universal soulmate.

Though I offer no exceptional wisdom, I give everyone what's needed from a best friend.

I connect with them on an existential level.

I make them feel better about themselves.

I don't sit in judgment of their actions, don't challenge or criticize their beliefs, and don't hurt their feelings or find fault with their conduct.

I do that behind their backs like other best friends do.

I take the opposite tack—with tact—instead, acting as a one-man support group to lead them to their future happiness.

If they need a *suggestion*, I make it. If they seek *encouragement*, I give it.

Suggestion and encouragement are close relatives of *influence* and *inspiration*, the very definition of an Agent of Fortune. But whether it exists or not, these attributes of mine enable me to toss out so many possibilities, so many insights that lost path-takers often don't know what hit them. Utilizing my full talents, I can almost predict their future.

I once used a snow globe as a crystal ball. It snowed the very next day.

I think that's why lots of people tell me they've never met anybody like me before.

Call me a mind reader if you must, but I know what you want just by knowing what I want. There's nothing uncanny about it. You can chalk up my intuitive powers to the human condition—the commonality of all mankind.

Okay, so maybe I don't have ESP. But I do finish my wife's sentences.

A little human understanding is all it takes to appreciate our fellow human beings. Sure, we may disagree about how to achieve what we want.

We might not even share the same tastes or values. But there's no doubt we all want the same damn basic thing.

To lead a happy and enriched life.

That's true whether you're a saint or a sinner, a CEO or an office clerk.

We're far more alike than most of us would care to admit. I wish everybody realized that. Then we could *influence* and *inspire* each other and everyone's life would be enriched.

Isn't that a world you'd rather live in?

If you're like me, your answer will be a resounding, "Yes!"

But sometimes, "No!"

35

I got out of the army by screaming "no!"
(How to live your life so others don't live it for you.)

THE WHIMS OF OTHERS once controlled me.

In the presence of friends, classmates, acquaintances, even total strangers, I had little say in how I lived. That's because I lacked the confidence to speak up for myself, having lost my mojo on the baseball diamond as a kid when my knee cartilage began to prematurely crumble.

Stripped of my ability to play the game in which I had excelled, I was left with no way to bolster my self-esteem. As a result, I withdrew into a protective shell that soon manifested itself as paralyzing shyness.

With my jaw now socially locked, I sat back and allowed others to tease me, abuse me, criticize me, and walk all over me. Without recourse, of course, as the next three single-paragraphed mini-stories below demonstrate.

When my best friend in grade school called me Katrina for a month, I had nothing to say.

When my rock band in high school kicked me out of the group for not being cool enough, I had nothing to say.

When a girl in one of my college classes patted my expansive belly and asked if I was pregnant, I had nothing to say.

That is no way to live. To become an independent, free-thinking human being, it became an absolute necessity for me to overcome my bashfulness and assert myself.

But how do you do that when you walk around like a *Kuni Leml* all day?[1] It left me with no other choice but to fight for the right to be me.

What was I after all? A man or a mouse?

It turned out I was a bit of both.

But writing solely as a man, the battle to be *me* began in my twenty-second year when I found an envelope from the Selective Service in my mailbox. Inside was the draft notice I had been expecting since I had dropped out of college the prior semester.

Leaving school wasn't the brightest decision I had ever made. It cost me sixteen class credits—and my Two-S student deferment. But I did it anyway. No big deal, I thought at the time. That's because my orthopedic surgeon had told me in high school that I'd be in a wheelchair by fifty.

Of course, I didn't know then that I'd be getting two future knee replacements that would reverse his prognosis. I only knew that before the war had become a divisive issue in America, I had nothing to worry about concerning Vietnam. I knew I'd be classified Four-F—government shorthand for...

One fuck.

I can't run.

Two fuck.

I can't kneel.

Three fuck.

I can't jump.

Four fuck.

I can't squat.

And I had a stack of X-Rays to prove it.

I've been irradiated more than a New York strip steak.

Complicating matters further, I was also conceived mere months after my father was exposed to a heavy dose of atomic bomb radiation at ground zero in Nagasaki. Do you have any idea how many mutated genes in my dad's DNA were passed onto me? I don't either. But more than one doctor has referred to my ultra-thick bones as "elephant bones."

How could a guy with elephant bones go off to fight in Vietnam?

Maybe I could in India or Africa—both countries have elephants. But Nam? Never! [2]

And that's why I wasn't concerned as I gathered all my medical records for the physical I'd be taking at the Army Induction Center in downtown Chicago.

In those days, recruits were herded like prodded cattle off to the slaughterhouse. They followed colored lines on the floor, moving from one test station to the next, where clinicians checked their vision, height, weight, reflexes, mobility, balance and conditioning.

At the tenth station, they stood the forty-some recruits side-by-side and asked them to raise their right hands.

"Repeat after me," some Sergeant began. "I—state your name—do solemnly swear…"

What the fuck! He's administering the oath.

"I will support and defend…"

This can't be happening. It has to be a mistake.

"The Constitution of the United States…"

I can't go to war. I can barely walk.

I stood there frozen, immobilized by impending doom, crippled by silenced timidity. But I just couldn't allow myself to roll over and sheepishly be led to slaughter. I had to do something fast. It was now or never—make or break—do or die time.

I let out a primal scream.

"NOOOOOO!!!"

It stopped the proceedings cold.

The Sergeant, his jaw now slackened and his eyes widened, shot me a disapproving glance. At first, I thought he would yell, like you'd expect an army Sergeant to do.

Remember Sgt. Zweitz from a few chapters back? He yelled at me a lot.

Surprisingly, the army sergeant didn't.

Instead, he gestured in a way that afforded me an invitation to speak. And I—now compelled to say something—*anything*—was forced to discover my long-dormant voice. I broke the uncomfortable silence with a stammer.

"S-sir, I-I can't go into the—uhh—army. I-I've got bad knees. I brought my medical records. But no-no-nobody's looked at them yet."

I garnered no visible sympathy from the other future inductees, but the Sergeant was quick to dispense some fatherly wisdom.

Calmly, he spoke, "A little advice, son. Next time, speak up sooner."

I've heard no wiser words since. Other than those of my dad—no scholar, he—who once defined life this way.

"If you don't ask, you don't receive."

I've learned many important lessons in life, but none as critical as learning how to speak up—and stand up—for myself. It's not easy to seize control of your own destiny. But you can't depend on anyone other than yourself to get the most out of your life.

So. always keep this in mind as the years go by.

If you don't live your life, somebody else will live it for you.

In other words, learn to steer if you want to sit in the driver's seat.

---

1. Kuni Leml was a simpleton in Jewish theater whose spoken name sounded as foolish and gullible as he was.)

2. Vietnam does in fact have elephants. So do fifty other countries in Asia and Africa. The rest of the world also has elephants, but theirs are behind zoo bars or under circus tents, other than the ones often found in rooms.

36

I got the better of a car salesman.
(How to turn the table on others.)

I DON'T LIKE TO haggle over the price of anything. But that doesn't mean I enjoy paying more than necessary.

So when my SiriusXM radio bill goes through the roof, I don't argue with the company. I just call and cancel my service.

I'm as shocked as anyone when they charge me half the going rate to keep me as a customer.

And when I purchase a new dining room table, I don't quibble about the cost. I just ask the proprietor if he or she accepts cash.

I can't help it if the shop owner then takes off another fifteen percent and charges no sales tax.

And when I check into a nice hotel, I never complain about the room rate. I just hand the front desk a box of fine chocolates as a token of my gratitude.

It's not my fault that they give me a free room upgrade, full access to the concierge room, and a basketful of goodies to thank me for my swell attitude.

Yes, I use lots of little tricks to help me get better deals. But nothing I do seems to work in car dealerships. It's just about impossible to come out ahead on a new car.

The odds against it are even higher if you're a woman. Here's the truth about that.

More than a quarter-century ago, I produced a news story for World News Tonight with Peter Jennings. It substantiated a study that proved women were taken for a ride when they bought a new car.

The report offended many females—and rightfully so. When they discovered they were paying more than men for the same car, they rose up angrily in unison.

What they failed to recognize, though, is that nobody—men included—ever gets a good deal on a new car. We may think we do. And the dealerships may lead us to believe we do. But I've bought or leased about fifteen cars in my adult life and I was positive I got a pretty good deal each time.

"It's just a hundred dollars over factory invoice," the dealer always says.

Then nighttime comes and I start mulling the numbers again. By three in the morning, I'm pacing the floors.

Counting dollars has the opposite effect on me as counting sheep.

Until it dawns on me that those car dealers got me again. I don't know how they do it, having never worked in a dealership. But all the advantages seem to lie in their favor. They hold all the cards, much like the odds in casinos are always stacked against the gambler.

Now I don't begrudge anybody's right to make a good living, and I usually forget what I pay for things as days pass. But I'd give anything to get the better of a car salesman. Just once.

That opportunity arose on the last car I leased in 2007.

Mindful that I wanted to keep my monthly payments the same as my previous vehicle's, I entered the dealership with a new strategy. I would tell the salesman up front that I didn't want to spend more than five hundred on payments.

The way I figured it, if I could get the same vehicle for the same price

I paid five years ago, I'd be getting a great deal.

It felt good when the salesman said five hundred shouldn't be a problem, and left for the sales manager's office to get final approval. Minutes later he came back with a big salesman grin cemented on his face.

"We can do it," he said.

I said, "Done deal."

We shook on it before he left to draw up the paperwork. I could hardly contain my joy that I had managed to come out significantly ahead on a deal.

I couldn't wait to tell my wife how crafty I had been.

Fifteen minutes later, he returned with the contract in hand. We started going over the details together. Everything looked fine until I reached the page listing the car payments. That's when I saw the five hundred dollars had crept up to five-eighteen a month.

I'm sure the salesman was hoping I wouldn't say anything, but I couldn't let something like that go unchallenged. There was a principle of honesty involved.

I unabashedly spoke up.

"I thought we agreed on five hundred dollars even."

He came back at me with a not-so-subtle attack on my manhood.

"Sir, you've got to be kidding. It's only eighteen dollars more a month."

He might as well have said eighteen bucks is pocket change. If you don't pay it, you're cheap.

I wanted to kill him one the spot, but had no ammunition.

I found a metaphorical bullet lodged in my brain. I did some high-speed multiplication in my head and quickly discovered that that piddling eighteen dollars a month spread over a five-year loan period would be an extra $1,080 that I'd be paying on the vehicle.[1] Quite a bit of *extra* pocket change for the dealership, don't you think?

My timing was near perfect when I replied, "You're right. It's only a measly eighteen dollars more a month. Why don't you pay it?"[2]

He had no answer.

Later that afternoon, I drove home in my new five hundred dollar-per-month Envoy. Unlike most other nights, I slept great that one.

I even dreamt of falling in love with lots of other women.

---

1. I've always been good at doing basic math in my head. Adding, subtracting, dividing and multiplying numbers without pencil and paper are my forte. Accordingly, I was nicknamed *Bowmar* by my college roommates, short for the old Bowmar Brain calculator. But even on my best days I can't do Geometry, Calculus or Trigonometry. Go figure.

2. My favorite rejoinder of all time took place when my ad agency boss boasted about how he once had a side job that paid him a hundred grand a year for doing nothing. Knowing my days at the agency were numbered anyway, I followed up his self-aggrandizement with this tarty retort. "If you were so good at it, how come you couldn't keep the job?" It got a few good laughs from everyone present. It also got me fired. But I couldn't have cared less. I had already lined up my new career at the *Today* show.

37

I shot the Bridges of Madison County.
(How to fall in love with another woman—and stay happily married.)

I WAS ROBERT KINCAID in the book, Clint Eastwood in the movie.

When I went to Winterset, Iowa, to shoot *The Bridges of Madison County* back in 1992, I played the role of leading man—a sensitive but manly freelance TV producer.

Or so I pretended.

My employer, ABC News, knew I was the right man or woman for the job. (Every other producer in the Chicago bureau was busy that day.) When the bureau chief called and asked if I was familiar with the best-selling book sweeping the nation. I said I knew of it, but hadn't read it.

He said, "It's a short, sappy love story. We need a news package for *World News Now* for tonight's airing. I have a camera crew coming in from Des Moines to meet you. You can read the book on the plane."

I bought the bestseller at the airport and read it from cover to cover on the short flight.

It turned out I was the one who was the sap. I sobbed uncontrollably upon reading the last few paragraphs.

I must have the genetic makeup of a woman. My eyes moisten way too easily.

Not wishing to embarrass myself, I tried to cover my face with a crossed forearm. It didn't work. Without any forearm tattoos to make me look more masculine than I am, my feminine side was left exposed.

Seeing how distraught I was, the flight attendant took notice and came down the aisle to check on me. I showed her the cause of my distress—the book. Nodding in all-knowing agreement, she gave me a sympathetic smile.

I fell madly in love with her at that moment.

But that was because the book had put me in a romantic mood, causing me to fantasize about running off with the flight attendant, though there was no way I could do that. After all, I was a happily married man who had left town for the day without telling his wife. I would have had a lot of explaining to do had I left Pam for a flighty fling.

Even if I had done nothing more than imagine it.

However, my faux affair did provide an interesting angle for the piece. With obvious parallels drawn between the protagonist in *The Bridges of Madison County* and me—Kincaid being the photojournalist and I being the broadcast journalist—I realized I could shape my own story with a life-imitating-art twist.

I wondered, what if a Winterset female resident and I fell madly in love, like Clint Eastwood and Meryl Streep had in the movie It would be a challenge, of course, since I've never been a leading-man sort of guy. Only catching the eyes of pretty, young females on my best days.

I'd probably win Mr. Congeniality in a handsome pageant.

But I was well aware of the opportunities this charade might create for me if I could pull it off and humor TV viewers in the process. That, I knew, had to be good for my career.

Plus, it gave me permission to flirt with other women.

Always a fun thing to do at parties, if you're invited.

A half hour after I landed, I pulled up to the Chamber of Commerce in the center of town and caught up with my crew. An attractive middle-aged PR woman representing Winterset greeted us at the front door. Upon introductions, she said, "I'm yours for the day. I can take you around to the bridges and help you any other way you might need."

I interpreted that to mean "You are such an attractive man that I want to be at your side all day."

I fell madly in love with her at that moment.

But I turned her down. Had to. It would have been tricky to get the other women of Winterset to pine after me with her hanging on to my every word. The crew and I needed the freedom to roam around town by ourselves.

I wasn't looking for love myself, though. I was simply on the lookout for wedding rings. When I'd see a married woman approach, I'd stop and ask for an interview.

About a half dozen agreed.

They had no clue what they were in for. No sooner than I got them to relax in front of the camera, I did an abrupt about-face and turned the interview upside down. I looked deep into their eyes and professed my love with a sincerity usually reserved for real-life lovers.

"I didn't expect it to happen when I came to town, but I've fallen madly in love with you."

The women played along. To have a network news producer in their town was cause for excitement, even though I was anything but exciting myself.

Next, the crew and I headed over to the covered bridges made famous by the book. Dating back to the 1880s, these bridges were a charming reminder of a pioneer spirit long gone. Their wooden planks, however, continued to live on as enduring love stories.

Carved into the boards were the romantic sentiments of thousands of lovers who had long favored these bridges. There were nostalgic reminders of first kisses, remembrances of prom dates long forgotten, and marriage proposals that may or may not have been accepted.

Seeing these carvings in person did not move me to tears like the book had. Love that ends well doesn't make me cry. It's love lost, as mirrored in the book, that opens the floodgates.

One woman, wondering what we were taping, stopped her car and got out. She was wearing a pretty print dress on a summery September day. I asked if I could record footage of her reciting passages from the book, thinking that I could use these excerpts to open and close the story. I positioned her off to the side of the road with one bridge slightly out of focus in the background. There she read:

> *"In that moment, everything I knew to be true about*
> *myself up until then was gone. I was acting like another*
> *woman, yet I was more myself than ever before."*

I fell madly in love with her at that moment.

Then I regained my senses.

I flew back to Chicago. Alone. When I arrived home late that night, I went to the kitchen for a bite to eat. There sat my wife, worried sick about where I had been all day.

I fell madly in love with her at that moment.

She, however, couldn't have cared less that I had shot the Bridges of Madison County that day.

She hadn't read the book.

But if she had known what role I had played in giving the story a romantic twist, she would have thrown it at me.

Like the Secret Service once threatened to do.

38

I got caught counterfeiting.
(How to laugh at your own misfortunes and cast them aside.)

IN ALL SERIOUSNESS, don't let the humor in my memoir fool you.

It's not that I don't take life seriously. I do. It's just that I see the humor in most situations. Even when those situations turn into big troubles as they invariably did in college when my brain often malfunctioned. A rapid review of past misdeeds confirms the above.

In 1967, I chose not to buy any of my college textbooks.

I was so proud of the two C's and two Ds I received.

In 1969, I used my first semester's college tuition money—about $175—to buy a new Gibson guitar. Two days later I grasped the concept that I couldn't attend classes without paying my tuition.

I decided to return it.[1]

It turned out to be the wrong decision after I failed two courses that semester.

Then, in 1970, I defaced the beloved Illinois Alma Mater statue by draping a peace symbol around her neck, much to the chagrin of campus authorities.

The photo appeared in the Daily Illini newspaper with the caption: Who did it?

Yes, it was me who did all of the above without thinking of the repercussions. But you must admit these *college admissions* of mine are kind of humorous.

And none is funnier than the time I got caught counterfeiting during my senior year. That's a pretty serious crime. I could have been charged with a felony and gone to prison. So why am I still laughing about it more than fifty years later?

Is it that funny to ruin one's life?

It can be.

If you ruin it right after you win the lottery.

But committing a serious crime is nothing to joke about.

Unless your wife is the judge and she doesn't want to support you anymore.

And prison is certainly no laughing matter.

Though it could be if Steve Martin is your cellmate.

But again, in all seriousness, it's not good when you're accused of breaking numerous counterfeiting laws of the U.S. Treasury Department. That is bad. Really bad.

Otherwise, two Secret Service agents in dark suits wouldn't have come a-knockin' at my door.

I was guilty as charged.

Guilty of exchanging fake money for real U.S. currency.

Guilty of transporting counterfeit dollars across state lines.

Before you condemn me, however, please allow me to preface both of the above charges by pointing out that I was unintentionally guilty in both cases. My objective wasn't to break those counterfeit laws for financial benefit but simply to discover whether the counterfeit money I possessed could pass for real money.

In that sense, my efforts were a social experiment of sorts, sort of like the time I outsourced a movie to India just to see if it could be done.

That made me *less* guilty of counterfeiting than of inciting a campus riot

189

my freshman year in college. But *more* guilty of counterfeiting than of masturbating the day I awoke to my first pubic hairs.

Nonetheless, I was technically guilty of all charges and facing a potentially dire outcome with nobody to turn to for help.

I couldn't confide in a priest.

I wouldn't confess even if I were Catholic.

I couldn't tell my parents.

Is that what we sent you to college for, you idiot?

And I couldn't tell the law enforcement authorities what they wanted to hear.

I ain't gonna rat out no campus radical for twenty bucks.

I could only plead ignorance. Which was the crime I was truly guilty of long before I learned how to think eight years later from a brother-in-law who helped me land a career in advertising.

But like I typed moments ago, my predicament wasn't merely a joke gone wrong. I had been caught counterfeiting, and the Selective Service was threatening to charge me.[2] Needless to say, I was concerned about my future, having never broken the law in any serious way before.

Sure, I'd been guilty of some questionable conduct in the past, like stealing nickels out of my mother's purse for candy bars.

The candy store banished me for buying too many.

Or convincing a fourth-grade classmate that the five-dollar bill he found on the street was fake.

You know, you might get in trouble if you keep that. Better let me hold on to it.

Or telling a blind date that I would call her when I had no intention of doing so.

Yeah, I had a really good time too.

But who isn't guilty of stuff like that?

And yes, there were dozens of other times when I was accused of being a bad, bad person.[3]

Once because I accidentally stepped on the back of a woman's shoe while she walked down Michigan Avenue in Chicago and ripped the high heel right off the sole.

When she stopped short, I rear-ended her. (Poor choice of words.)

Once because my boss's son uttered an anti-Semitic remark.

I told him I was Jewish. He said it was mean of me to say that.

And once because a female Korean driver thought I had given her the finger.

My mistake was to motion her past my car with my middle digit in a parking lot.

All that being written, none of these misbehaving deeds were illegal. The punishment doled out for each was negligible.

Other than the fact that I have to live with myself.

In contrast, exchanging fake money for legitimate currency was no petty crime. It was counterfeiting. I may have thought it was funny, but the Feds thought otherwise. Instead of ascribing my obnoxious behavior to that of a stupid, immature college student, they were treating it like I had broken into Fort Knox.

As is often the case, the truth lies somewhere in the middle. I'll let you be the judge of whether my criminal act was serious or humorous. Or possibly both.

Below is the inside skinny of the case for and against me.

The Feds were dead serious when they accused me of accepting twenty counterfeits one-dollar bills from a campus radical at the University of Wisconsin.

I was dying of laughter when I saw Richard Nixon's face where George Washington's belonged.

The Feds were dead serious when they threatened to prosecute me to the full extent of the law.

I was dying of laugher at the idea of spending the rest of my life in prison for accepting obvious counterfeit money.

The Feds were dead serious when they asked why I hadn't handed over these counterfeit dollars to the authorities.

I was dying of laughter after Walter Cronkite said on the news that these phony bills worked in dollar change machines.

The Feds were dead serious when they said I walked—with premeditation—to the dollar bill change machine at the university snack bar.

I was dying of laughter when I fed the machine twenty counterfeit singles and got back sixty valid quarters, forty authentic dimes, and twenty genuine nickels.

The Feds were dead serious when they asked me to return the twenty bucks.

I was dying of laughter when I paid them back with the exact change I got from the dollar change machine.

And that's how this whole affair went down.

Today, I'm dead serious when I write that there's a fine line between what's funny—and what isn't. I've crossed that line many times, but I advise you not to do the same. You might find yourself in deep doo-doo if you do that.

Though I might laugh at your troubles, it's not lost on me that my sense of humor may be a defense mechanism I use to save myself from a truth too painful to handle.

Of course, that suggests the joke has always been on me.

It just dawned on me I might have a learning disability.

1. The same Gibson guitar I bought in college for $175—an amount that covered my whole semester's tuition back in 1968—now sells for about $1,300. All things being equal, that provides us with a fairly accurate estimate for what a semester of college should actually cost these days. A far cry below the $11,349 that in-state colleges now charge on average. (As published in U.S. News & World Report magazine, September, 2021.)

2. The Secret Service not only protects all present and former U.S. Presidents and their families, they also enforce the counterfeit laws of the U.S. I have no idea why they pull this double-duty. It must be one of the secrets of the service.

3. I've always been an easy target. In high school, my history teacher frequently sent me out to the hall—once wrongly accusing me of flinging a balled-up piece of paper at another student sitting a few rows in front. The teacher eyed every guy with suspicion before singling me out. Why? I'll tell you why. Because "born smilers" like me are often unjustly accused and punished. We've been abused for centuries. I believe it began with court jesters, whose heads got lopped off for saying the wrong thing. (In jest, of course.)

39

I beat Simon.

(How to excel at something without being born great.)

Simon says,
tell me the truth.

        Okay, I'm an
        idiot savant.

Simon says, explain
the idiot part.

        I don't comprehend
        everything I hear.

And the savant part?

        I can multiply 250x37
        in my hea—
        Dammit, got me again.

I'M OFTEN FOOLED by Simon Says.

The game moves too fast for me. That's because my reaction time to spoken language isn't quick enough to keep up with all the words whizzing by.[1] I suppose that's why I became a writer. You're able to think before you type.

This same state of confusion also causes me to stammer sometimes. My thoughts often come faster than my brain can process the words. And my comprehension is a half-beat slow, making it problematic for me to respond in a timely manner.

That's the idiot in me.

I attribute my dumb nature to a learning disorder I must have had as a kid. In the 1950s, schools didn't test for any—and nobody knew they had any. The probability that I'm walking around with that same learning disability today is high.

I've learned to cope with this intellectual deficiency, though. Over the years, it's become a major part of who I am. If not a welcome part, an acceptable part. Acceptable, because there's another wrinkle in my brain that makes up for dumb me.

That's the savant in me—the rare talent I have that helped me beat Simon. Not the kid's game, *Simon Says,* but a Simon more in tune with my innate gift.

This Simon, popular in the 1980s and still in toy stores nowadays, is the electronic memory game of musical tones and flashing lights. I beat this Simon two times and probably would have whipped its ass more times if I hadn't lost interest in the game. But I still remember the first time I won.

First times of everything are hard to forget.

If you're unfamiliar with Simon, the game is divided into four quadrants—each featuring a different colored light and musical note. To beat it, you need to recall the random order in which the four separate musical tones and accompanying colored lights turn on and off thirty-two times. What makes the game more troublesome is the lights and tones gain speed as the game progresses. To untrained ears and eyes, it's chaos.

It goes without saying—that's why I'm writing it—that it took a tremendous amount of concentration on my part to focus on the task at hand.[2] But that, in and of itself, was not a winning strategy.

This was:

Before I pressed a single button, I simplified Simon.

First, I ignored Simon's four musical tones. I determined they were superfluous to winning. As a former musician with a good ear, I know that non-melodic music with no differentiation in rhythm is impossible to remember.

Then I *uncolored* the four colors. What do colors have to do with anything? Other than looking pretty in the dark when lit up, there was no intrinsic value to them.

That freed my mind to concentrate on the sequential order in which the thirty-two lights flashed. It goes without writing that few people are capable of keeping that straight in their head, myself included. I needed a simpler strategy that would make memorization a whole lot easier.

As easy as one… two… three… four.

I found it by numbering the four colored quadrants of the game clockwise from one to four. As they lit up in their respective numbered sections, I committed the first seven numbers to memory—e.g., 1-1-2-3-1-4-2—before repeating the process four more times.

Why did I choose to remember groups of seven numbers rather than six? Or eight? Or nine or ten? Because seven of anything is very memorable. A good example is phone numbers.[3]

Or for that matter, the seven deadly sins, the seven colors of a rainbow, the seven notes in a major musical scale, the seven wonders of the world, the seven dwarfs—and 7UPs.

By breaking the game down this way, I reduced the hectic nature of Simon. It made winning no more complicated than memorizing five phone numbers in twenty minutes. I presume that was quite savant of me.

But remember, I'm also an idiot.

Yin. Yang.

Either. Or.

Translation: Everyone has strengths and everyone has weaknesses.

As an example, you may be good at sports, but suck at music.

Or be great at math, but stink in chemistry.

The point is, nobody is great at everything, and nobody sucks at everything. The secret is to find out what your strengths are and run with them.

The three things I'm best at are daydreaming, composing and writing. This is why I spent a good portion of my life doing what I did. I honed those talents and used them to carve out a profession.

And so can you if you commit the following paragraph to memory.

Why compound life by leading with your weaknesses rather than your strengths?

Why run uphill when you move faster and easier downhill?

Why swim against the current when you swim quicker and farther with it?

Common sense says we're all better off developing our strengths before our weaknesses. At least you'll end up good at something. That's what happened to me. My life might have gone downhill if I hadn't led with my strengths.

Maybe I would have discovered I was pretty good with numbers and become a cashier.

Hmm, no, thank you.

I have no doubts I wound up happier the way I did. It made me a touch more savant and a smidgeon less idiot.

"Says who?" Says Simon.

"Says me," says Rick.

Now onto something that should have gone unsaid.

---

1. It's not my fault that I can't translate English in my head as quickly as other people. I have a brain processing issue that makes it harder to decipher spoken language. I've had this affliction forever, but didn't discover it until I had my hearing tested in my late sixties. Conclusion. The longer you live, the more you discover the truth about yourself.

2. I refer to myself as a "lost man." Not because I get lost when I drive or follow directions, but because I get lost in thought for hours on end. In this near-hypnotic state of mind, I concentrate so intensely that I become uncommunicative. My wife and children will attest to that. Shake me. *I'll feel nothing.* Talk to me. *I'll hear nobody.* All systems are running on autopilot. My wife says she's never seen anything like it—likening my deep concentration to an epileptic seizure. (Far from it.) But I'm not alone. Plenty of others are like me, including writers, musicians, athletes and traders. By the way, as a "lost man," I broke the record for most baskets sunk at the ESPN Zone in Chicago in 1997—a record I held for two years, though I can barely dribble. Except out of the side of my mouth, that is.

3. The "Magical Number Seven" psychological experiment in 1956 showed that the maximum number of things a human being can easily memorize in any category is seven. Anything above that number can create confusion. And that is why phone numbers—along with dwarfs, wonders, sins and rainbow colors—come in sevens. Source: Psychology Today magazine, November 19, 2012.

40

I tested the limits of good taste.
(How to say the wrong thing at the right time.)

"I DID IT, I DID," I said.

Dr. Seuss, I'm not. That's fortunate. Because what follows should never be read by innocent eyes, nor heard by naïve ears, nor uttered by guiltless lips—the lips being a central theme to this story. But before I go on, allow me to fill you in on the backstory, so you'll have an honest and objective account of what I did.

The following material is rated PG.

In 1996, I went to Eureka Springs in north-central Arkansas, home to a well-known artist colony—and a furniture design company named "Mixed Nuts." Two female designers ran the business which manufactured a line of brightly colored kids' furniture constructed from corrugated cardboard.

Their creations were smart, inexpensive and sturdy. There only failing was that nobody had heard of their brand. I was brought in to change that—by producing and distributing a video news release that would publicize their company nationwide.

The strategy was to show how strong and durable their furniture was in comparison to more costly wood furniture. I demonstrated that product benefit by hiring a bunch of kids to put the corrugated cardboard beds, dressers, chairs, tables, and desks through the wringer. I'm happy to report that the children were unsuccessful in destroying any of the furniture.

Ecstatic with the results—and relieved from the stress of a long day's shoot—the clients' mood lightened. They, and their contingent of seven other female personnel, were ready to party.

The following material is rated PG-13.

Though I had budgeted for a client dinner, the owners of Mixed Nuts would hear none of it. They insisted on treating everyone—everyone being the nine women and me—to an extravagant dinner at an artsy-fartsy restaurant.

Multiple cocktails included.

I mention the liberal consumption of alcohol thing to let you know I wasn't drunk when I did what I did. Otherwise, you'd assume I must have been blotto at the time. But I don't need alcohol to loosen my tongue—the tongue being another central theme of this story.

I do it quite well sober.

The following material is rated R.

In contrast, the women at the table were giddy from hard liquor, predisposing them to any and all amusements emanating from my mouth— the mouth being another central theme of this story.

In the past, I've gotten away with bloody murder when blurting out shocking words. That's because I have a soft, gentle-looking face, and smile a lot. I also have (had) curly hair. Overall, I look as safe and cuddly as a Teddy Bear, making me a fan favorite of mothers everywhere.

If not their daughters.

However, being likened to the least dangerous inanimate object on the planet isn't the worst quality a man can have. It allows me to safely interject topics that usually don't come up in ordinary conversation. Like the bold sentiment I said to my future wife in 1973. *(See the footnote in Chapter 20.)*

The only reason she didn't divorce me then was because we hadn't yet been introduced.

So when I found myself sitting at the far end of the table in mixed company with the Mixed Nuts entourage, I couldn't think of one good reason not to let loose with a jaw-dropping, inappropriate remark.

The following material is rated NC-17.

One word popped into my head. For a moment, I controlled my urge to say it, thinking it might be in poor taste. But I've never been someone to back away from a challenge.

I held up my index finger and, with lips half-parted, delivered a pregnant pause. The women shushed and, in anticipation, leaned forward to listen to what I was about to say. Then, with all eyes upon me, I quietly uttered one innocent four-syllable word.

"Cun-ni-lin-gus."

Dead silence.

Uh-oh. What the fuck did I just do?

Then a sudden burst of laughter. The woman adjacent to me raised her hand and said, "I'm in."

This time, belly laughter.

I gave all the women my most endearing smile and shrugged sheepishly like a young boy caught with his hand in the cookie jar. I had successfully tested the limits of good taste and male survival in a female world.

Care to know how I got away with saying what I said?

Being a Teddy Bear is one thing; being a lascivious Teddy Bear is another.

It's because I knew my audience. These were boisterous, fun-loving, potty-mouthed businesswomen who could handle pretty much anything I could dish out—something my dear wife can't. But she's not reading over my shoulder as I type right now, so allow me to reiterate…

Rick, you idiot, don't test your luck.

"Cunnilingus."

I apologize to all you modest and prudish women reading this filth. But I just can't help myself. As for the ladies at Mixed Nuts, they responded favorably to the dirt spewing from my mouth.

Later that night, we all went out to sing karaoke. While walking, one woman took my arm.[1] Was it my imagination? Or did she have a touch more bounce to her step?

I tried to put my wife out of my mind but couldn't. I never can. So let me state in black and white what the lesson is here. When it comes to communications, everything matters.

Sex matters, race matters, nationality matters, socio-economic status matters, and marital status matters. So always size up the crowd before you voice one syllable.

That said, I'd like to offer a few words of warning to all of you cocksure gentlemen out there. I am not an amateur communicator—I repeat—I am not an amateur communicator. I am a pro's pro. I know how to get away with things other men can't. If you say the same stuff I've said out loud, you could be seriously injured in the groin area or charged with sexual harassment.

Oh, and one more cautionary piece of advice about the central themes of this story, gentlemen, namely your lips, tongues and mouths—the three tools of oral—*ahem*—communications.

The following material is rated X.

Please refrain from using the *expletive* derived from cunnilingus—the most hated word of females everywhere.

As for what I said, I'm pretty certain the women understood it for what it was. Cute and harmless Rick just acting cute and harmless.

That's how I got away with it. But as I wrote at the top, that was in 1996.[2]

Today, I'd be insane to try it.

---

1. No marriages were destroyed in the telling of this story.

2. The Statute of Limitations on my indecent language ran out in 2006.

41

I drove my crazy uncle temporarily sane.
(How to avoid judging a book by its cover.)

"SHHH," I WHISPERED, trying to calm my baby sister Jill down.

The doorbell had just rung, sending the two of us scampering up the stairs to my bedroom closet. The Bogeyman had arrived for supper, but no way were we going to dine with him.

Even if he was our uncle.

I can't remember the day Uncle George came into our lives. It may have been when I was about six. But by nine, I knew him for what he was, a paranoid schizophrenic who had been in and out of mental institutions since World War Two.

His doctors said he wasn't dangerous, but I never bought that diagnosis, having witnessed his many severe meltdowns over the tiniest of perceived slights.

Though his medications helped control these periodic mood swings, they resulted in a more Lurch-like than Leslie-like uncle.

Fearful of being around this crazy man as a child, I chose to ignore him until I was a sophomore in high school. That's when my uncle relapsed and was once again institutionalized.

One night soon after, I woke up to sobs emanating from my parent's bedroom across the hall. I assumed it was my mom crying, but then a deep, guttural groan arose, and I realized it was my dad. I knew something awful was up because I had never known him to cry. In the darkness, I lay silently in bed as he spoke about Uncle George.

"He was always peculiar, even as a kid. So damn sensitive all the time."

Those weren't the best words for an oddball kid like me to hear. It made me wonder if I was going to turn out like Uncle George.[1]

Then, thinking the kids might be eavesdropping, my parents' voices promptly softened. My mother ended this tête-à-tête between husband and wife with a barely audible, mystifying whisper.

"I think it was the incident that broke him."

The sentence left me hanging in the dark.

Incident? What incident?

This was the first time I had heard what might have triggered Uncle George's craziness. I fell asleep wondering what horrors could have befallen him.

I was reluctant to bring up the topic the following morning at breakfast, but out of concern for my own well-being, I couldn't hold back.

"Dad, why did Uncle George go crazy?"

And that's when I first heard the story.

My father told me Uncle George had suffered a nervous breakdown during his stint in the army, brought on by battle fatigue. The trauma had caused him to throw an ill-advised punch at a senior ranking officer, resulting in a court-martial—the straw that broke my uncle forever.

It sounded like a reasonable explanation to fifteen-year-old me. But with each passing year, I began to question the logic of the story.

How does a twenty-four-year-old man wind up a paranoid schizo-phrenic because a few stripes were ripped from his uniform?

It didn't make any sense.

It was also a lie—a lie that sheltered my sisters and me from the dark nature of the universe. But you can't protect children forever.

I was well into adulthood when my dad finally confessed to another dark chapter in Leslie family history. This one was about how my grandmother wasn't really my grandmother. She was actually my grandpa's second wife. Evidently, my real grandmother had died five years before I was born when she fell out an apartment window she was washing.

And that's where this story would have ended if not for the discovery of a long-lost second cousin whose mother was among the living. That's when I discovered my grandmother didn't fall out of any window.

She threw herself out one in 1942.

My Grandma Anna's suicide aroused my curiosity.

Was this the *incident* my mother had spoken of in bed?

Was this why my uncle went nuts?

It didn't seem outlandish to think a fragile twenty-two-year-old might shatter from an event like that.

To see if I could shed any further light on his illness, I wrote the military and requested a copy of my uncle's service record

It confirmed what I had speculated. There was no mention of battle fatigue—*my uncle had never seen combat*—nor any mention of a court-martial—*he had been honorably discharged.*

On the back page were multiple notations of my uncle's mental issues dating back to basic training, including an extended stay at the Kentucky State Hospital, a military installation for soldiers suffering from psychiatric illness.

That meant my Uncle George was either crazy—or starting to go crazy—*before* the war. Not after as my father had led me to believe.

The final typewritten sentence at the bottom of his discharge papers provided me with the answer I sought.

Mr. Leslie hasn't recovered from mother's suicide.

With that revelation, the final piece of the puzzle had fallen into place. I had finally learned the truth about Uncle George.

Though by then, I didn't feel any closer to him than I already did. That's because I had grown fond of my uncle forty years earlier when we shared a brief, tender moment together.

A moment that changed my views about him—and his mental illness—forever.

I was practicing guitar in my bedroom when my dad walked in. Troubled over something, he said, "I just got a call from Aunt Marian." I knew what that meant. It was a sign that my uncle had once again gone off the deep end.

"George threatened some tenants in his building," my dad continued. "We may have to commit him again. Can you go there with me? He might be dangerous."

But my uncle was anything but dangerous when we got to his apartment. He was sitting in a docile trance, ignorant of our presence. He had a far-off look in his eyes, smiling at who-knew-what.

"He's hallucinating,' my dad said.

Soon, a couple of healthcare workers arrived, placed my uncle in a straitjacket, and strapped him to a gurney, before wheeling him out the door.

Suddenly, Uncle George's head bolted upwards, the cartoons in his head having subsided.

Staring straight at me, free of all delusions, he gave the saddest look a sane person could make.

I saw shame on his face—shame that his nephew had to see him like this.

And he saw shame on my face—shame that I had dismissed him till then.

Seconds later, his demons returned. And he let out a deep moan. I walked over to rest my hand on his cheek.

"Shhh," I whispered, trying to calm my uncle down.

I dared not blink. Out of fear I'd soon be facing monsters myself.

---

1. When mental illness runs in your family, you often question your own sanity, if not the sanctity of your beliefs. I've reflected on both since I learned the truth about my uncle and grandmother. Sometimes I think my bizarre behavior—and freakish imagination—is a sign that I'm losing it. And so might the fact that I wrote this book. The closer I get to finishing it, the more I fear I've typed page after page of gibberish. And my memoir/how-to book is nothing more than a horror story authored by a demented person. (Help me, please. I need to escape these parentheses.)

42

I interviewed two of the scariest men in America.
(How to make dangerous people surrender to you.)

DURING MY YEARS AS a TV producer, I interviewed about a thousand people, including many famous ones.

Comprising the shortlist were former President Gerald Ford, filmmaker Oliver Stone, TV star Oprah Winfrey, actors John Cleese, Rick Moranis and Dolph Lundgren, hall-of- famers Willy Mays, Ernie Bank, Billy Williams, Dominique Williams, Dikembe Mutombo and Alonzo Mourning, welterweight champion Sugar Ray Leonard, Nobel Laureate Leon Lederman, legendary Cajun fiddler Dewey Balfa, and pop psychologist Dr. Joyce Brothers. Collectively, they all made me feel more significant than I really was.

Rubbing elbows with the rich and famous is pretty cool, you know.

My proudest achievement, however, came when I interviewed two of the toughest, meanest men you'll ever meet. Both appeared in a documentary-style corporate video I produced for Mobil Oil in the mid-nineties. The first was the CEO of Mobil Oil—a man likened to a tyrannical king who ruled over his company with an iron fist.

And the other gentleman, if I dare type it, was the leader of the Crips—

a cold-blooded killer in charge of Los Angeles' most notorious street gang.

Though both men stood tall on opposite sides of the law—as well as the business world—they shared a lot in common. Both could put the fear of God in you, (though Satan might be a more applicable description).

And both were empire builders, driven by a similar cause: To grow the bottom line of their organizations, whatever the cost.

For those with limited knowledge of euphemisms, "cost" is a euphemism for being fired or murdered. or both.

Interviewee #1: Mr. Mobil CEO

When Mr. CEO agreed to be interviewed, his corporate *yes-men* told me I had to get in and out fast. The man was so dreaded that grown men and women shook in his presence, often resulting in cottonmouth—a condition that can turn sensible sentences into blithering nonsense. Something I sometimes suffer from as well.

In both writing and speaking.

Explains trouble have you might with book my reading.

Be that as it may, Mr. Mobil CEO's appearance in the video lent a crucial ingredient to the production: It sent a message that this particular project was significant enough to warrant his presence.

In a pleasant turnaround from what his cronies had advised, Mr. Mobil CEO, like many others have done before, immediately succumbed to my line of questioning as we rolled tape.

Actually, two thirty-minute tapes.

The man wouldn't stop talking. His face lit up as I probed his consciousness about the state of the world circa 1994. Speaking with an authority only attained by immense power, he reasoned that you can't create an economic boom at the local level—referring to blighted neighborhoods around the country—without generating economic growth globally.

An hour and a half later, I walked out of his office with a smiling CEO beside me. It caught everybody in the hallway off guard. Were the *yes* men happy? My guess was yes.

One scary interview down, one more to go.

It was onward to South-Central LA. Where the Watts community was celebrating the grand opening of a new minority-owned—and Mobil-financed—service station and mini-mart.

I was shooting the festivities there when none other than the leader of the—*gulp*—Crips rolled into the station. Since I had no idea who he was. I unwittingly began to make my way to his car. But I only got three steps before my client pulled me back by my shirttail with a warning.

"Be careful. That guy is the leader of the Crips."

Leader of the Crips? Oh, crap.

It didn't stop me, however. Though Crips is shorthand for crippled (that often being the state of their wounded adversaries), I made my way over, figuring all was safe in daylight.

Unless I did something stupid.

But it wasn't stupid to include Mr. Crips Leader in the production. Of course, I couldn't identify him in the video. That would have been in bad taste.

But because only neighborhood locals would recognize who he was, I determined his cameo appearance would work as an endorsement of the project. And, in so doing, provide protection to the service station, and spread goodwill within the wider Watts community.

Interviewee #2: Leader of the Crips

When I approached Mr. Crips Leader's car, he rolled down his window. I respectfully filled him in on what we were doing, and asked if he would answer a few questions. He said he was happy to oblige.

In words other than "happy to oblige."

I positioned the camera so nobody could see the tattooed teardrops running down his face,[1] and struck oil with my first question about the lack of economic development in South Central LA.

Cautious of how he might respond, I leaned a few inches back from his car in case he pointed a gun at me. Instead, he shot from the hip with an *unexpected* reply about neighborhood development which made him sound more like a Ph.D. candidate than a gang leader.

What's going on here, I asked myself, as Mr. Crips Leader drove off? Was I wrong to judge these men too quickly? Was it possible both he and Mr. Mobil CEO were better men than I had believed? They each had smashed all expectations of *who* and *what* they were.

But I'd have to be naive to believe either man was anything other than *what* he was.

Here's my explanation for their outstanding performances that day. Each man had fallen prey to something more powerful than they were— the video camera. Get one up and running and people will always place themselves in the best possible light.

Maybe a camera on every street corner isn't a bad idea after all.

At a minimum, it would stop nose pickers from doing their probing in public.

Now before you finish reading, let me leave you with one final thought.

We're all in this together. So act accordingly.

Hey, anybody got the time?

---

1. A well-known hip-hop artist in Chicago told me that teardrop tattoos represent the number of opposing gang members you've killed in the hood. Mr. Crips Leader had numerous ones on his face. I was too nervous to count them all.

43

I know how to get rid of an eye tic.
(How to recover quickly from a near-nervous breakdown.)

TIC. TOC.

I once developed—*tic*—an annoying eye—*toc*—tic.

It fluttered every few—*tic*—seconds like clock—*toc*—work. Drove me—*tic*—crazy for over a month—*toc*—just like it's irritating you—*tic*—reading about it—*toc*. It seemed like the twitch—*tic*—would never go away—*toc*. It was turning me—*tic*—into a nervous wreck—*toc*—so I saw my doctor—*tic*—to check it out—*toc*.

And guess what? He cured me on the spot. Not with shots, meds, or treatments of any kind. But with a few well-chosen words that freed me from the vice-like grip of an ever-beating eyelid spasm.

Dr. Wolfe was one smart doctor.

He should have had his own TV show. He was quite a character.

I know you're dying to know what wisdom he imparted that worked such wonders, so I won't keep you waiting. He examined my left eyelid up close before delivering this enigmatic prognosis.

"Your tic will go away once you accept, you're going to have it the rest of your life."

As you know by now, I'm not big on abstract stuff. But that little mind trick of his turned out to be one hundred percent accurate. I put it into action that afternoon, and by morning I awoke tic free. It was like a battery inside my eyelid had gone dead. Silenced. Forever. Never had an eye tic again.

Nor have I had any panic attacks, fake brain tumors, chronic fatigue syndrome, or any other diseases of the mind since then. (Though I do welcome a healthy bout of depression now and then.

Otherwise, I wouldn't know if my anti-depressant was working.

But what a godsend *acceptance* turned out to be. It was the first time my mind had taken itself *off* itself—if you know what I mean—and started thinking about things other than itself.

I'm not sure I even know what that means.

So let me explain the good doctor's treatment in layman's terms.

Acceptance works like an annoyance-blocker. It pushes disturbing thoughts out of your head and stops you from dwelling about your disorders. That's how my doctor turned me into an assassin of psychosomatic diseases in the seventies. The ammunition I used to kill them was the simple act of *acceptance*, as taught by Dr. Charles K. Wolfe. Doctor of doctors. Once imprisoned.[1] Long gone from this Earth.

But living on through me.

I am Dr. Wolfe's disciple, having learned firsthand the results of his "tic" work. I continue to spread his medical gospel, touting its central selling point.

Acceptance helps your mind heal your mind, freeing you of neuroses.[2]

Think of it as a placebo for a better life.

For decades, I've been free of crippling anxieties, debilitating worries, nagging aggravations, forehead-tightening stresses, and tortuous internal conflicts. I find it amazing that I can cope with nearly anything simply by accepting everything.

Until I forget it's even there.

That's why I liken the mechanics of *acceptance* to the deafening roar of passing trains. I grew up across the street from a commuter train line. Every hour, two trains would rattle my home. When my family moved there, we couldn't hear ourselves speak each time a train passed. But as the months passed, we adjusted to the noise and the tracks quickly quieted until we heard nothing all day. I find it remarkable what the human mind can do if it just accepts its circumstances.

Unconditionally.

Without question or guarantee.

Today, I pretty much accept anything—and everything—that comes my way. And I'm better off for it.

I accept my diminishing role in the universe, so I'm not afraid to die.

I accept that I have an imperfect life, so I don't worry if things go wrong.

And without exception, I accept the existence of germs, having once eaten a chocolate donut that had fallen frosting-side down on the sidewalk. It landed between the cracks atop an anthill, but I couldn't have cared less. Still looking scrumptious, I picked it up, dusted off the filth and the ants, and ate it.[3]

Look, I was only five years old then, so don't even think of criticizing me.

I'm pretty sure the germs were good for my immune system anyway, but I doubt the chocolate did much good for all my future maladies in need of cures.

What I wouldn't give to reverse my myocardial infarction.

Undo my diabetes.

Unclog my pisser.

Reattach my bicep muscles.

Return my rotator cuffs to normal.

Unlock my unbending fingers.

Or turn my neck sideways once again.

I live with these ailments, as millions of other aging Boomers do. But *acceptance* helps me tune out the worst of their symptoms. I've been doing it for close to fifty years now. Most days, I feel okay.

And on days I don't, I wash my aches and pains away with a glass or two of vodka or a medicinal gummy bear, causing me to run through my house like a high school fullback and breaking free of tacklers and diving into the end zone.

Touchdown.

That's not *acceptance*. That's me falling to the floor for the third time this year.

But should you follow the recommendations of Dr. Wolfe and Mr. Leslie, a few words of caution. This mind game, if you're not careful, can play funny tricks on you. Please use your new power wisely. The human brain cannot be trusted in full, because it doesn't always have your best interests at heart.

It lies to you on occasion.

It can fool you into thinking you have a great voice when you sing in the shower, hallway or garage.

It can make you feel like you're more valuable to your employer than you are.

And it can convince you to write a book that doesn't just tell all, but tells way too much.

Like sharing my memory of a mother indifferent to the welfare of her son.

My most humiliating experience ever.

---

1. Dr. Wolfe wound up in prison for tax evasion. I'm not sure breaking the law was a smart thing for him to do. But I believe in giving credit where credit is due. Here's a silent shout-out to Dr. Charles K. Wolfe, now deceased, forever remembered.

2. What do you call a Jewish man without neuroses? An uncircumcised orphan.

3. There are up to forty million viruses and eleven million bacteria in every cubic foot of air you breathe. I learned that on a trip to the "clean room" at NASA. So a little spit, phlegm or dirt on your food isn't going to kill you.

44

I was marooned in junior high.
(How to survive life as a social outcast.)

ON MY FIRST DAY of junior high, I was marooned on a desert island, engulfed by bloody red sunsets and blue twilit skies—ironically, the two primary colors that make up the color maroon.

So when I write that I was *marooned* in junior high, what I'm really writing is two things.

First, that a lot of my classmates ignored me.

And second, that the color maroon had something to do with it.

Before the maroon industry sues me for libel, please note that I hold no grudges against the color itself.[1] Only the overabundant use of it. Too much of any color can become obnoxious, just like too much of anything can make you want to throw up.

Even ice cream and Oreo cookies.

But I don't live life according to the law of diminishing returns—an economic principle that isn't a law at all. Just a wordier way to apply financial considerations to the philosophy of architect Mies van der Rohe— the "less is more" guy.

As in less maroon, more popularity.

How silly that reads.

But in junior high, popularity was what every kid sought because the more popular you were, the more desirable you became to the opposite sex.

How level-headed that reads.

It goes without saying that a little sexy foreplay with a pretty girl of similar age will work wonders for a boy's self-worth. There were two contributing factors that killed off any chance of that happening to me.

The clothes I wore. And the mother who bought them.

I'll get to my clothes momentarily, but first, a warning to young male readers about moms in general.

Never trust your mom.

She will mislead you.

She will betray you.

She will destroy you.

I have a forgiving nature, so let's skip the time my mom offered me a slice of coffee cake prepared with a cup of coffee grounds in place of the freshly brewed cup of coffee the recipe actually called for.

Let's forget the day she embarrassed me by tossing a baseball farther than I could at a mother/son baseball game.

Let's erase my memory of the day she burnt the tip of my nose with an errant tip of her cigarette.

And jump right to the part where she clothed me totally, completely, entirely in maroon.[2]

Only a moron would wear maroon everything.

There's only one possible explanation for that kind of mistreatment. And that's that mothers will destroy their sons even if they love them.[3]

Which is why my mom, with no input from me, bought me a new set of clothes for the first day of junior high. I've never been much of a clotheshorse, but even I knew something was *off* about all the matching maroon clothes draped across my bed.

What was my mom thinking?

This outfit might have been appropriate for a teenage girl, but it certainly wasn't a cool look for a twelve-year-old boy.

Oh, dear God, I'm going to be color-coordinated head to toe.

I stared at the maroon pants, maroon shirt, maroon belt, maroon socks, and maroon loafers laid out before me. These clothes would determine my junior high social standing on the same day new classmates were met, new friendships developed, and impenetrable cliques forged among those who—well—*click.*

Too obedient to argue with my mother's fashion sense, I dressed and headed downstairs for breakfast, where my mother gave my ensemble the once-over—and me her verbal seal of approval.

"My, you look handsome today."

Say something, Rick. Don't be a dope. Change the course of your life now.

I can't remember the face I made to my mother, but I absolutely remember the discomfort that set in as I walked the three blocks to school. A short conversation developed between my gut and me. It was one of the few times in the history of mankind that both gut and intellect synced up in perfect harmony.

> Rick: I'm so embarrassed.
> *My Gut: I'm going to be the laughingstock today.*
> Rick: Maybe nobody will notice.
> *My Gut: I'm going to be hard to miss.*
> Rick: I'm such a dork.
> *My Gut: I'm such a dork.*

Of course, my gut and I never speak aloud to each other. We just read each other's mind to appear normal on the outside. But on the inside, well, that's a whole other story.

As for that first day of junior high, I wish I could type that everything turned out fine. That I met a lot of cool kids, got tight with the in-crowd, and was invited to a bunch of make-out parties.

But I knew I was a loser before I walked through the school entrance that day—a fact substantiated seconds later by a classmate who, upon eyeing me in the hall, shouted, "Nice garb, you idiot."

Or something to that effect.

There's no further need to say I spent junior high on the sidelines. Neither is there any point in complaining about it. Not everyone deserted me. Many other unpopular kids in junior high, undergoing allegorical maroons of their own, wound up in the same shipwrecked boat as me.

Seriously, only two committed suicide before their twentieth birthdays. (Not kidding.)

The majority survived just fine, as I did in the end.[4]

I acquired a bunch of new friends, had lots of fun sleepovers, and laughed heartily on most days.

And though I had no cute little girls in my life to build my self-esteem, I did have a steady right hand, and the mind-blowing ability to conjure up sexual fantasies with naked females of all ages at a moment's notice.

Even the high school teacher who flunked me for cheating on a test was the object of my affections.

I effed her plenty in my imagination to get even.

And so was my friend's mother, who once welcomed me into her home in bra and panties.

Oh my, Mrs. G.

But that was all so long ago.

(Insert pleasant body shudder here.)

Before I get turned on, let me switch to another subject—the clothes I wear today. I obviously shy away from weird colors, vertical and horizontal stripes, and anything else that could be considered embarrassing.

That leaves me with a wardrobe stocked with jeans, hoodies, sweaters, tees, six untucked white and blue dress shirts, and black slip-on shoes.

Women my age seem to like my look. They say it makes me look years younger than I am. But it's not lost on me that these grandmothers were once mothers themselves.

So you can't trust them either.

Frankly, I learned long ago to trust only my own instincts.

---

1. I also have an aversion to burgundy, maroon's close cousin.

2. I should brief you on "The Turquoise Man." I saw him at the movies one night wearing turquoise everything. Hat, shirt, pants, belt, socks and shoes. He also muttered to himself throughout the film. I suspected it was his mother's fault that he had turned out odd. I couldn't help but think that I could have turned out the same way if my mom hadn't had the good sense to choose a better color combination than turquoise. Thanks for that, Mom. RIP.

3. Why did so many Jewish men born in the early twentieth-century drop dead of heart attacks at a relatively young age? Because their mothers accidentally poisoned them with the chicken schmaltz they used in their cooking. They dared to call it love, when it was really manslaughter.

4. Ten years after donating my maroon clothing to Goodwill, my mother bought me a blond corduroy leisure suit with flashy gold zippers everywhere. She believed it would be a good look for me when I performed on stage. Maybe Elvis could have pulled it off in Vegas, but I wasn't about to wear that outfit in public. It hung unworn in my closet for years until I gained a few pounds, forever making it unsuitable for wear. Too embarrassed to donate it to Goodwill, I tossed it in the garbage bin at a nearby convenience store.

45

I told my boss to take out a loan for my raise.
(How to know when to go all in on a bet.)

I ONCE GAMBLED big on myself.

I mean real big. Like out-of-a-job big. Whole-paychecks-lost big. Mortgage-foreclosed big.

If my wife had been there to see it, she would've cut off my cajones.

In the mid-eighties, annual ten percent pay raises were the norm for good writers. But insulting to anybody performing well beyond average.

That was the case with me. I found my ten percent raise offensive, and rightfully so. I had just come off a banner year as the agency's most productive writer,[1] personally responsible for thirteen of the fourteen TV commercials my creative group had produced.

That total represented one-quarter of the agency's output for the year, including the "best commercial to come out of the agency in years," wrote the advertising columnist in the Chicago Tribune.

Excuse me for presuming my salary would go up commensurate with my one-man-wrecking-crew performance. When it didn't, I couldn't contain my displeasure.

"Four thousand?" I snapped back in reply. "That's all I'm getting?"

I had said this to my boss, David Fairman, who mere seconds earlier had slid a folded sheet of paper across my desk with the amount of my raise scribbled inside.

His secretive flair had led me to believe I was about to receive some happy news. When I saw that it fell well below expectations, I followed up my initial shock at his lowball offer with an aftershock of my own.

"It's not good enough," I said.

If my wife had seen me do this, she would've slapped me silly for displaying such bad manners.

Under normal conditions (from a normal copywriter), that would have been the wrong thing to say. After all, my boss wasn't expecting me to complain about a ten percent increase. But I often say and do things that shouldn't be said or done, like I did five chapters back with a tableful of tasty women.

Though it's never been officially diagnosed, I believe I suffer from *Roulette's Syndrome*—a condition that causes me to say inappropriate things at the most inopportune of times while putting everything I have at risk.[2]

It left me with no choice but to go for broke.

"I'm worth more than four grand," I said.

Fairman responded to my ultimatum with some harsh language of his own.

"Sorry, that's all the agency can afford. We didn't have that good a year."

Though Fairman was indeed a fair man, I doubted his "poor-mouthing" version of the truth was the honest-to-God truth. But I had no comeback to his agency's "shortage of funds" excuse short of calling his bluff. But that might have led to something stupid coming out of my mouth like...

"I quit."

Oh, God, no.

Or...

"I'm going into real estate then."

Me? On commission? No way.

Or…

"Then you're going to have to go to the bank and take out a personal loan to pay me."

Whoa. Did I say that?

Yes, I did.

Fairman left my office in silence. Uh-oh.

If my wife had seen that, she would've heaved butcher knives at my head.

Was my response over the top? Definitely. But it wasn't irresponsible.[3] Without a doubt, I had pushed my request for a more satisfactory raise to the limit. But I was holding some valuable cards myself.

I knew it would cost the agency far more to replace me than to give me what I wanted.

Besides, if you don't get what you're worth when things are going well for you, you're never going to get it. And if you're never going to get it, you might as well leave.

That sound business axiom I just typed in the previous paragraph implores you to quit when you're in a dead-end career. It goes like this.

Mr. and Ms. Millennial, go where you can succeed.

And that's why I went all-in.

I had to.

There were clearly no assurances I'd have another big year. What if the quality of my work took a nosedive? Then what? Here's what. I would have been axed like everybody else in advertising is if they stop coming up with good ideas.

It's not like I was being greedy, either. I just wanted another three or four extra thousand—a trivial amount for a company billing over two-hundred million dollars, but enough to make me happy.

Enough to make me jump through future hoops at work.

And enough to help me buy a better car, go out for a decent family dinner every week, and switch from frozen to fresh orange juice in the morning.

I can't say I was amazed when Fairman walked into my office a few hours later with a grin he couldn't quite suppress. It signaled better news to come. I was going to get more money. Lifestyle-changing money. But how much? He didn't waste any time telling me.

"We're going to double it," he said. "Is that better?"

Before I spoke, I smiled on the inside.

"Yes, much better," I said.[4]

If my wife had been around, she would've discovered I sometimes know what I'm doing.

If there's a lesson to take away from my twenty percent pay raise, it would be two-fold. Never sell yourself short.

Or, for that matter, overestimate your worth.

I did neither. And got exactly what I deserved.

As did the anchorman who got on my wrong side eight years later.

---

1. I had a banner year only in the sense that I was the most productive writer at a mediocre ad agency. I always considered the vast majority of my commercials to be humdrum ideas. When I wound up a CLIO judge in 1985, I knew my own commercial entry was undeserving of advertising's highest award. I voted against myself.

2. In 1994 I produced a corporate news package that aired in its entirety on Good Morning America. The following day I got a call from WKBW, the ABC affiliate in Buffalo. The news director asked if I'd be interested in being their feature reporter. As much as I loved the idea, it was for half the money I was making. At forty-six, it would have been reckless to give up everything I had— and take on a dicey new challenge. Money, job security, and family do count for something, you know. But immaturity is the thing I miss most about being young.

3. When I was given power of attorney over my uncle's and aunt's financial matters, I gambled big on their behalf. I invested all of their money in Apple stock at twenty dollars a share. At the time they had enough savings to pay for another two years of assisted living. I was hoping to extend their future care beyond that so they could avoid going on Medicaid. The stock quadrupled over the next year, making my stock purchase a smart investment. However, when my broker found out what I had done, he admonished me. "Are you crazy?" You could be held responsible if you lose their money." The following day I sold all of the Apple stock, and have watched it go up and up since. I no longer use the same stockbroker.

4. The four thousand-dollar raise I was offered in 1984 is equal to about twelve thousand today. Using that logic, the extra four thousand dollars I got was a sizable chunk of change. Though my wages and bonuses continued to rise over the next two decades, I never earned bragging rights on any of my W-2's.

46

I tricked an anchorman into paying my office rent.
(How to get the last laugh on somebody who thought they got it on you.)

DON'T EVER GET ON my wrong side.

I can be tricky as hell when I'm wronged. Especially when someone is as nasty to me as Pill was.

Pill is not Pill's real name. But it rhymes with *Pill.* As do *Ill and Will*—two well-suited names for a person like Pill. Since I don't wish to embarrass celebrity newspeople—*they can sue you*—I won't share his actual name. But if you know your anchormen well, you might figure out who screwed me.

And who I screwed back.

Once a popular local news anchor and the former host of a morning network TV show, Pill was nothing like he was in his professional life.

Far from the sober journalist everyone presumed him to be, he was, in fact, a fraud—closer in demeanor to Ted Baxter of the old *Mary Tyler Moore* show than to present primetime news anchors like Lester Holt, David Muir or Norah O'Donnell.

Somehow Pill managed to keep his true character hidden from the public.

As an insider, however, I worked with Pill quite a bit. He was a giggler, a goofball, and an overgrown man-child. But he was also born with a gift—a deep and earnest voice custom-made for TV news.

No, he wasn't Ron Burgundy, but close.

In the early '90s, I had taken on a new partner, a Yale-educated up-and-comer bound for big success. He had worked with Pill on a bunch of pre-produced cable TV documentaries and had managed to bring that business into our new company. We didn't get paid a lot for the work, but the income provided us with steady cash flow—account receivables any business would love to have.

Invoicing was always my favorite part of owning a business.

But it came at a cost. We had to put up with Pill's obnoxious behavior in exchange for that regular monthly income.[1]

I considered this arrangement a reasonable trade-off, until the day Pill and I went on the road together to tape an original episode of the show. It was about the Kennedy assassination and would include interviews with former president and Warren Commission member Gerald Ford and filmmaker Oliver Stone, who had just released his movie *JFK*.[2]

That's when Pill revealed his true nature.

The initial plan was for Pill and I to meet at Ford's office in Rancho Mirage, California, to conduct the interview with the former president. Then I would drive alone to Marina Del Rey for an interview with Stone.

However, Pill showed up late for the impatient Ford. After an hour, I made an executive decision to start the "Q and A" without him. When Pill finally arrived, we switched seats so he could finish up the interview.

Then Pill asked if I could give him a ride back to the airport. Though I was running behind schedule and had a two-hour car trip ahead of me, I kindly agreed.

But there was one little snag. Being unfamiliar with the area, I didn't know how to find my way to I-10 West from the Palm Springs airport.

Lest you've forgotten, gentle readers, GPS systems—a life-saving contraption for directionless network news producers like me—hadn't yet been invented.

Pill told me not to worry. He said he was acquainted with the area and would point me in the right direction once we got to the airport.

A half-hour later, when I pulled up to the terminal curb, Pill hurried out the door without addressing my concern and headed straight to the entrance. Out of desperation, I screamed out the passenger side window.

"Hold on, Pill."

Though he already knew what I was going to say, Pill spun around and arched one of his dark, bushy eyebrows with feigned curiosity.

"How do I get to 10-West from here?" I asked.

And that's when Pill revealed his true nature. He gave a carefree shrug and said, "Hell if I know."

Hell if I know?

I couldn't believe he had said that to me. This man was a class A jerk. I scored his flippant reply a 7.5 on the *Rickster* Scale—high enough to merit some sort of reprisal.

But what?

Not wishing to sacrifice a profitable business relationship for a momentary verbal salvo—as satisfying as that might have been—I let Pill's remark slide.

And I would have gladly left it there if Pill hadn't let loose with one of his high-pitched giggles. It was irritating as hell. And no way to treat a fellow human being.

(Look, I may be a nobody, but nobody likes to have his or her nose rubbed in it.)

I gave Pill a piece of my mind. (Not out loud only in thought.)

Well, know this, cocksucker. One day I'm going to screw you back.

In actuality, one day turned out to be two days. That's how long it took me to get even with Pill.

When I returned to my office in Chicago, I called a nearby post-production facility known more for finishing corporate videos than for doing broadcast TV work. They had significantly lower rates for editing and computer-generated 3-D graphics than the posh post-production houses we were presently using.

Before my negative encounter with Pill, I wouldn't have dreamed of using their services for our documentaries, but I was fighting mad and wanted to see how much our work—along with our promise of more to come—would be worth to the owner.

It turned out to be a lot.

When I offered the owner a chance to edit a weekly cable network news show in exchange for a show credit, he cut his hourly editing rate in half.

I hesitated.

He then sweetened the pot, tossing in 3-D graphics for free.

Again, I hesitated.

And then came the game-changer—the cherry on top, so to speak. The owner sealed the deal by tossing in free office space in his building, saving us tens of thousands of dollars in annual rent.

But how did that screw Pill?

Here's how: Prior to production, we had signed a contract with Pill to split all profits down the middle. But contracts often have loopholes, and this one was no exception. Our agreement with Pill didn't permit us to hike any of our post-production costs without his approval, but it didn't preclude us from lowering those hard costs without telling him.

While billing him the old, more costly rate.

That meant we would earn more, and he would earn less, on every production we did together—and would do in the future.

And that's how I screwed Pill.

And the best part is Pill never found out what I had done.

True story.

Something I can't say about the next.

---

1. Pill's clownish behavior was nothing like my own tomfoolery. I've never used my silly nature to rag on anyone but myself. As for the self-deprecating humor in this book, I use it to charm people and make myself more likable. You should see the sorry-looking Stan Laurel face I'm making right now. How could anyone hate someone like me? (Please don't answer that.)

2. Let me tell you a thing or two about Oliver Stone and his film *JFK*. As good a director as he was, Stone was no less a fraud than Pill. When I interviewed Stone at his office, he had to run into the hall after every question to ask his female entourage what to say. How did I know that? Because I heard everything they talked about through the closed door, including the affirmation that Stone knew nothing about the assassination, and had pretty much made his whole storyline up.

47

I lied to my psychiatrist.
(How to get even with people who find you boring.)

BEING AN OUTLIER—but not the out-and-out liar many readers might imagine me to be—I've always had a difficult time fitting in with other men. Put me in a roomful of guys and I clam up. If I had to guess why, I'd write that I never learned how to speak the universal language of men.

I can't talk about business or financial investments.

And I have no interest in cigars, cars, camping, golf[1] or gambling.

Confession: I was the only dad at a father-son fishing outing who wouldn't pick up a worm.

Oddly enough, I'm the bipolar opposite with women. I've always gotten along fine with them.

As long as I'm not pursuing them.

Just how big of a problem was my male phobia? Let's sum it up this way. My anxiety around men was of greater concern to me than my nightly teeth grinding. But it fell short of grounds to kill myself.

All things being equal—even if no things are truly equal in life—I thought it best to alleviate my fears by seeking the help of a mental health professional.

Two of them in fact.

I started with a female psychologist who told me she couldn't help me after my first visit. Evidently, she didn't want me as a patient. I'm pretty sure it had something to do with my lack of wet dreams during puberty.

Or, far more likely, my raising the topic with her.

If you can't remember them, what's the point in having them?

"I was cheated out of a major part of my adolescence," I told her.

She referred me to a male psychiatrist. I saw him one time as well, though the topic of sexual arousal never came up.

Dr. Baker seemed competent enough. He did the job a shrink is supposed to do, helping me blab away about myself. But ten minutes into our first session, he committed a psychiatric no-no.

He yawned.

How could that be, I pondered? I had always considered myself engaging. I couldn't fathom how a professional listener could find my gut-spilling confessions pedestrian, though admittedly, on the Brief Psychiatric Rating Scale (BPRF)[1] of sicko-psycho behavior, my failure to fit in with other men might have been somewhat bland in comparison to men in sanitariums.

In short, I wasn't a serial killer.

Though I once sat next to one.

I've never suffered from delusions of grandeur.

Except when I made a diving, game-saving catch in Little League with two outs in the ninth.

And I'm pretty sure I don't hallucinate.

Though I once wished I did after seeing a woman crap in the aisle of a grocery store.

I suppose that makes me more normal than I sometimes think I am. So maybe I shouldn't have been alarmed when my psychiatrist found my confessions dull. But, really, was it necessary for him to yawn right in front of me?

Truthfully, I never actually saw his yawn. Dr. Baker had deftly cupped his hand over his mouth to hide it, demonstrating how well-trained he was in such maneuvers.

But I saw through it. Literally, through it. I saw his jaw muscles tighten around the edges of his mouth and sensed a subtle change in air pressure as he sucked all the oxygen out of the room. The result? The room suddenly deflated and—*whoosh*—just like that, the shrink had shrunk my ego.

Correct me if I'm wrong, but aren't psychiatrists supposed to do the opposite? You know, restore your confidence and build your ego up.

I've always been a sensitive person, not just to my needs but to those of others as well. If somebody does something wrong, I usually cut them some slack.[2] That's the kind of person I am—always respecting the feelings of others, (especially those I like).

Which is why I didn't like my psychiatrist at that moment. He, of all people, should never have hurt my feelings. I would have been well within my rights to say something like, "Yeah, I'd like to nap too, but I'm a little busy right now."

Trying my hardest to avoid confrontation, I carried on as if nothing had happened. But something *did* happen. My goal for the session had changed. I was no longer seeking Dr. Baker's advice. I was out to make myself more interesting.

I started lying to him.

I told him some of my darkest secrets—secrets I didn't even know I had until I shared them with the doctor. I can't recall what they were. But if you'll allow me a little leeway, I'll provide some examples of tales I might have easily blabbed about to show you how fascinating my lies can be.

First fib.

235

Doctor, I got my roommate's Siamese cat stoned on marijuana in college. I balanced him atop the picture rail molding that ran a foot below the ceiling. I left him there for five minutes, motionless, trapped, with nowhere to go. The cat was never the same after that.[3]

Doc, how can I live with myself?[4]

Second fib.

Doctor, my older sister locked me in a dirt-floored, pitch-black cellar filled with spiders when I was four. She told me the bogeyman was going to get me. I cried hysterically, but she wouldn't let me out. Soon after, my fear of spiders grew into a fear of worms, flies, moths, ants and cobwebs.

Doc, how can an unmanly man like me fit into a group of testosterone-laden he-men?

Third fib.

Doctor, I was run over by a bicycle when I was three. I was lying down in an alley when some kid rode over my face.[5]

Could that be why I'm a teeth grinder now?

By appointment's end, my psychiatrist said I would benefit from three sessions a week.

Three sessions? You've got to be crazy, you yawning money-grubber.

I made the appointments anyway. But the following day, a Saturday, I called *Dr. Mind Fuck's* office and left a message on his voicemail.

I began with a big yawn, followed by, "Oh, hi, Dr. Baker. I'm canceling the appointments I made yesterday. I'm feeling much better now. Thanks for your help."

Funny thing was, I did feel better. And, after realizing how ridiculous it was to fear men, I never *shrank* away from them again.

Except for odd ones like me.

Now onto the end. The bitter end. Almost.

236

1. The Brief Psychiatric Rating Scale (BPRS) is a tool mental health clinicians and researchers utilize to measure symptoms like anxiety, depression and psychoses.

2. Years ago, I scratched a woman's car pulling out of a parking space. It was my fault, but the woman went bonkers on me. I gave her my insurance info, assured her everything would be okay, and sped away to a friend's house. When I got there, I told him what had transpired— how this crazy woman had gone ballistic over a minor accident. He stopped me mid-sentence and said he had already heard the story. It turned out the woman was his wife's friend. And she was in his house at that very moment. Somewhat of a troublemaker, he wanted to introduce me to her. I begged him not to do it, because I didn't want to cause her further anguish. That is so me on the outside. So not me on the inside.

3. In my defense, I've always hated cats. They eat mice and lick you. *Yuck!* Far worse are the allergens they put in the air. So, when my college roommate bought a cat, without asking my permission first, I had to save myself. To this day, I hate myself for what I did to "Pussy." I haven't mistreated any other animals since, unless I count the goldfish I once flushed down the toilet, the ants I've stepped on, and the mosquitos I've slapped.

4. If I were me, I'm not sure I'd like me either.

5. Like George Washington, I cannot tell a lie. That being the case, all three of my "lying" examples in this chapter actually occurred. See how interesting I really am. Even the lies in this chapter were honest-to-goodness true stories.

Epilogue

I barely survived the ending of this book.
(How to write off your life and screw the IRS)

I'M STILL ALIVE. Sorry. Please accept my apologies.

I know I promised readers I would die at the end of this book as an incentive to read all forty-seven chapters of *I Pissed in Some guy's Bottle Of…*.

But when I predicted the end of *me*, I only meant that all lives must eventually come to an end. Not that I—Rick Leslie—would die right after I put the finishing touches on my manuscript.

Book endings like that don't occur every day, you know. How spooky that would have been if I had prophesied my passing at the beginning of my book. Squeamish is a word that comes to mind. It also would have turned my memoir into a self-authored obit, possibly making my book more attractive to publishers of the occult.

I myself would never buy a book written by a guy willing to die to make his book a better read. In my opinion, only a sick, depraved individual would pull a stunt like that.

But life being what it is—most often out of our control—I somehow managed to type the final period to my manuscript without doing myself in, resulting in new hopes and dreams for myself that go far beyond the average age of male hoping and dreaming.

(Read: Death of A Salesman.)

And then the accident happened.

The first officer arriving on the scene looked down at me and said, "You know, people die in car crashes like these."

The way I felt, I didn't doubt his word, but I think he only said it to cheer me up and let me know how lucky I was to be alive.

Again, I apologize for that.

But he was right. I was lucky. The spinal cord injury I sustained in the crash resulted in temporary paralysis. But like my orthopedic surgeon later said, "It could become permanent with one little misstep."

Six vertebrae required fixing. Scary stuff. But following surgery, the prognosis wasn't half bad. With five rods and ten screws implanted in my now fused neck, I stood half an inch taller, making me the oldest guy to ever grow up.

Another side effect of the accident was a loss of energy and stamina. Unable to type—or think straight—for more than a few minutes, I put my memoir on hold for over a year while I put all my efforts into recovery.

Though I had finished the third draft of my manuscript an hour before the accident, I felt the need to rewrite the original epilogue gracing these pages in favor of a new ending that expressed my *near-ending* more clearly.

And that brings me to the here and now.

Today, I'm able to do most everything I could before. Just at half the speed and twice the effort, thereby creating the illusion that time has sped up because I've slowed down.

According to my definition of the *Theory of Relativity,* it will now take me ten minutes to live out the next twenty astronomical years, barely enough time to take a shower. Something I don't need to take, since I took one mere seconds ago yesterday.

Hmm. That was kind of funny for an old white man's joke.

Yes, my sense of humor remains intact.

Excluding all talk of constipation.

I don't find that amusing anymore. And I'm sure you wouldn't either if you had gone eleven straight days without going following surgery. The condition caused my blood pressure to drop, my bedroom to spin, my mind to go blank, and my face to smash into the floor, followed by a second ambulance trip to the ER.

Believe me, that one was no vacation either.

Though I suppose it could be likened to taking a trip to a dude ranch.

That is my way of segueing to the subject of toilets. Like many people, I think best when sitting on one. There's something about the relaxation of the sphincter muscles that opens up the mind to fresh new ideas. And that's where I sat when I came upon a new master plan for my book.

If not for the car crash, I'd be harboring the same old, unrealistic hopes and dreams I had before—get published, sell a million copies of my book, and live happily ever after. But how realistic is that? The odds of aliens existing are better.

In the event every publisher thinks my book is stupid, I've got a backup plan. To implement it, I only need to sell one copy because the second I sell a single book—even if that person doesn't read one page—I will have become a real author.

The author of me.

Meh

Okay, so maybe I'm not that big of a deal, but I'm pretty positive my book will entitle me to modest celebrityhood at my nearby morning cafe.

"Good morning, Mr. Leslie," the man behind the counter might say. "Your coffee's on me today."

What? No pastry? I might reply indignantly.

But that's nothing compared to what else lies ahead. As a real author, the IRS will allow me to write off all research expenses in the authoring of my next book. I already have the name of the sequel.

I Pissed on The IRS Code. ©2028.

Catchy, isn't it? And it won't have to be well-written either. Then again, who says this book was?

I dedicate this memoir to all my English teachers who made me use commas where I didn't want to use them.

Since the sequel will also be about everything that happens to me over the next few years, everything I do in the future will be tax-deductible. No piddling deductions like I used to get as a songwriter, jingle singer, adman, news producer or storyteller. This time I get to deduct everything.

It could be a vacation to Hawaii in Chapter 8.

Or a ride in my new BMW 6 Series Convertible in Chapter 32.

Or the lakeside mansion I'll be buying in Chapter 56.

The IRS might not like my plan, but I dare them to come after me. If they track me down, it will become a chapter in the book.

I outwitted the IRS.

(How to keep most of the money you make.)

And I'll hire a lawyer to sue them. Who cares if I lose? What are they going to do? Put me in prison? I'll just write about that and write off my penitentiary expenses.

One quality pickaxe, $49.

Upon reflection, the car accident might have been the best thing that could have happened to me. If all goes well, I should be able to write off my entire life. Until I'm written off all together. Then I'll write off all my funeral expenses. Just because I'm me.

And nobody else.

As you've probably already concluded.

Bonus

A Reader's Lullaby.
(How to properly thank your readers.)

Thanks for being good readers
Thanks for being well read
Good night to you all
It's time now to fall
Asleep curled up in your bed
Asleep curled up in your bed

Yeah, sure, right! Like I'm supposed to believe you read the entire book.

www.ingramcontent.com/pod-product-compliance
Lightning Source LLC
Chambersburg PA
CBHW051139120626
46547CB00012B/872